THE IMPORTANCE OF

Louis Armstrong

These and other titles are included in The Importance Of biography series:

THE IMPORTANCE OF

Louis Armstrong

by
Adam Woog

Lucent Books, P.O. Box 289011, San Diego, CA 92198-9011

Library of Congress Cataloging-in-Publication Data

Woog, Adam, 1953-
    Louis Armstrong / by Adam Woog.
        p. cm.—(The Importance of)
    Includes bibliographical references and index.
    ISBN 1-56006-059-X   (acid-free paper)
    1. Armstrong, Louis, 1900-1971—Juvenile literature.   2. Jazz
musicians—United States—Biography—Juvenile literature.
[1. Armstrong, Louis, 1900-1971.   2. Musicians.   3. Jazz.
4. Afro-Americans—Biography]   I. Title.   II. Series.
ML3930.A75W66   1995
781.65'092—dc20   94-296
[B]   CIP
                                                                      AC MN

Contents

Foreword

THE IMPORTANCE OF biography series deals with individuals who have made a unique contribution to history. The editors of the series have deliberately chosen to cast a wide net and include people from all fields of endeavor. Individuals from politics, music, art, literature, philosophy, science, sports, and religion are all represented. In addition, the editors did not restrict the series to individuals whose accomplishments have helped change the course of history. Of necessity, this criterion would have eliminated many whose contribution was great, though limited. Charles Darwin, for example, was responsible for radically altering the scientific view of the natural history of the world. His achievements continue to impact the study of science today. Others, such as Chief Joseph of the Nez Percé, played a pivotal role in the history of their own people. While Joseph's influence does not extend much beyond the Nez Percé, his nonviolent resistance to white expansion and his continuing role in protecting his tribe and his homeland remain an inspiration to all.

These biographies are more than factual chronicles. Each volume attempts to emphasize an individual's contributions both in his or her own time and for posterity. For example, the voyages of Christopher Columbus opened the way to European colonization of the New World. Unquestionably, his encounter with the New World brought monumental changes to both Europe and the Americas in his day. Today, however, the broader impact of Columbus's voyages is being critically scrutinized. *Christopher Columbus,* as well as every biography in The Importance Of series, includes and evaluates the most recent scholarship available on each subject.

Each author includes a wide variety of primary and secondary source quotations to document and substantiate his or her work. All quotes are footnoted to show readers exactly how and where biographers derive their information, as well as to provide stepping stones to further research. These quotations enliven the text by giving readers eyewitness views of the life and times of each individual covered in The Importance Of series.

Finally, each volume is enhanced by photographs, bibliographies, chronologies, and comprehensive indexes. For both the casual reader and the student engaged in research, The Importance Of biographies will be a fascinating adventure into the lives of people who have helped shape humanity's past and present, and who will continue to shape its future.

Important Dates in the Life of Louis Armstrong

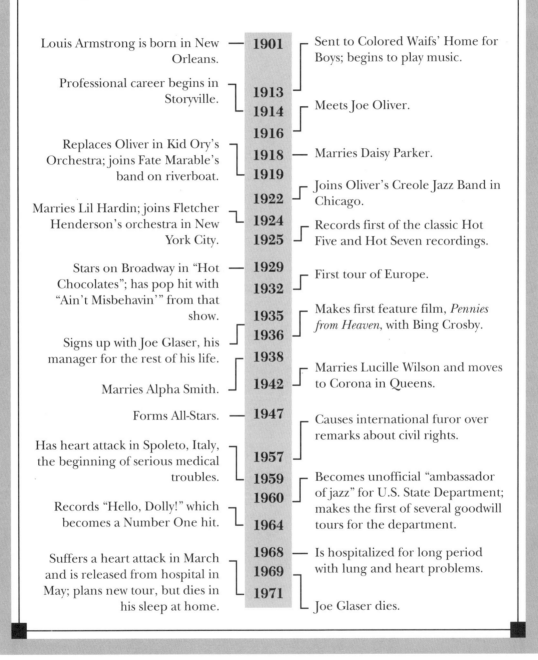

1901 — Louis Armstrong is born in New Orleans.

1901 — Sent to Colored Waifs' Home for Boys; begins to play music.

1913 — Professional career begins in Storyville.

1914 — Meets Joe Oliver.

1916

1918 — Marries Daisy Parker.

1918–1919 — Replaces Oliver in Kid Ory's Orchestra; joins Fate Marable's band on riverboat.

1922 — Joins Oliver's Creole Jazz Band in Chicago.

1924 — Marries Lil Hardin; joins Fletcher Henderson's orchestra in New York City.

1925 — Records first of the classic Hot Five and Hot Seven recordings.

1929–1932 — Stars on Broadway in "Hot Chocolates"; has pop hit with "Ain't Misbehavin'" from that show.

1932 — First tour of Europe.

1935 — Makes first feature film, *Pennies from Heaven*, with Bing Crosby.

1936 — Signs up with Joe Glaser, his manager for the rest of his life.

1938 — Marries Alpha Smith.

1942 — Marries Lucille Wilson and moves to Corona in Queens.

1947 — Forms All-Stars.

1957 — Causes international furor over remarks about civil rights.

1957 — Has heart attack in Spoleto, Italy, the beginning of serious medical troubles.

1959–1960 — Becomes unofficial "ambassador of jazz" for U.S. State Department; makes the first of several goodwill tours for the department.

1964 — Records "Hello, Dolly!" which becomes a Number One hit.

1968 — Is hospitalized for long period with lung and heart problems.

1969–1971 — Suffers a heart attack in March and is released from hospital in May; plans new tour, but dies in his sleep at home.

1971 — Joe Glaser dies.

This Music Called Jazz

"Louis Armstrong is the beginning and the end of music in America."
Bing Crosby

"The bottom line of any country is, what have we contributed to the world? And we contributed Louis Armstrong."
Tony Bennett

"It's all folk music to me—I never heard no horses playing it."
Louis Armstrong

Since its first appearance, the music called jazz has defied definition. It is many things to many people. Is it improvised music? Swing? Hot scatting and slow ballads? Fusion? One of America's great contributions to the world? Jazz is all these things, and more.

Over the last century, jazz has evolved from its origins as a rough entertainment for honky-tonks and speakeasies into a sublime art form with a thousand variations. Along the way, it has affected virtually all other major forms of twentieth-century music, from classical to rock. And it continues to change and grow.

Whatever jazz is, one thing is certain: Louis Armstrong was, and is, its once and future king. The standards of imagination, technique, innovation, and sheer love of playing that Armstrong set have never

Arguably the greatest jazz musician of all time, Louis Armstrong captured the hearts of millions of fans around the world with his imaginative music and universal message of goodwill.

been matched. He had an impact on the music's development and growth that is still felt. As another giant of jazz, Miles Davis, once remarked, "You can't play anything on a horn that Louis hasn't played."[1] Because of his influence on jazz, and because of jazz's influence on other forms of music, it is possible that Armstrong did more to shape music than any other single person in this century.

"Ambassador Satch"

In his later years, he became much more than a musical genius—he was a lasting symbol of what America meant to the world. As "Ambassador Satch," the U.S. State Department's unofficial ambassador of goodwill, Armstrong carried his message of freedom and love through music to millions of people worldwide. ("Satchmo" was one of Armstrong's many nicknames.)

It didn't matter if he was playing for royalty, politicians, working folk, or prison inmates—he brought the same robust energy to every performance. For many, the very word "America" was synonymous with his unmistakable sound and presence.

What made Armstrong so special? There have been other giants in jazz. He was not the first brilliant jazz performer, and he was not the last. Nor did he invent jazz all by himself.

But Armstrong was a great popularizer. He took the rich mixture of music he'd grown up with in New Orleans, filtered it through his own imagination, and presented it to the world. The audience always came first, and he never played down to them. He always played in a way that everyone could understand and like.

Armstrong was also a brilliant technician. His early recordings were the first great recorded jazz solos. Even later, when lip problems prevented him from playing high-flying solos, each note was perfectly placed. According to pianist Teddy Wilson:

He had no weak point. . . . I don't think there has been a musician since Armstrong who has had all the factors in balance, all the factors equally de-

Whether he was playing for royalty, working folk, or prison inmates, Armstrong never let his audiences down. He always played with the same energy and enthusiasm that helped make him famous.

Louis by Any Other Name

Louis Armstrong had many nicknames, and there is disagreement over whether his first name was pronounced "Louisss" or "Louie." Gary Giddins, in his biography, Satchmo, *reflects:*

"Some books and articles call him Daniel Louis Armstrong. No one seems to know where the Daniel came from. Armstrong said it wasn't part of his name, and his baptismal certificate backs him up.

You can start a fight over how he was addressed by friends. The Louis faction ('Hello, Dolly, this is Louisssss, Dolly' the man sang), can get downright rude about those who pronounce it Louie. He wasn't French, they point out. But many friends and at least two wives called him both.

The safest and by far the most common form of address was Pops, which is how he addressed everyone else—though in letters he would refer to male friends as 'my boy' and to himself as 'your boy.' As a kid with a large trumpeter's mouth, he earned many nicknames, including Dippermouth or Dip, Gatemouth or Gate, and Satchelmouth or Satch. This last, unwittingly corrupted by a British journalist (Percy Brooks), survived as Satchmo.

Insiders will tell you that no one ever called him that. No one but the man himself, who loved the name, and a hundred million fans who loved him."

veloped. Such a balance was the essential thing about Beethoven, I think, and Armstrong, like Beethoven, had this high development of balance.[2]

His singing eventually took on an equally important role in his performances. This unlikeliest of voices—a hoarse, gravelly, but expressive croak—has influenced generations of jazz and pop singers. Armstrong virtually invented the art of jazz vocals.

He also had a gift for turning the dullest material into gold. This gift is one of the true marks of artistic genius. Over a long career Armstrong recorded thousands of songs, many of them utterly forgettable—except that his interpretation made them special. Jazz writer Gary Giddins notes that Armstrong knew "that no song could diminish him, and that he could lift most songs far beyond their earthly calling. Though he appreciated quality . . . he was undaunted by junk."[3]

Armstrong the performer became rich and famous. Armstrong the man took the fame in stride. The honors from govern-

Armstrong plays a few licks on his horn for his wife Lucille during a visit to the Giza pyramids. Armstrong believed that he was put on earth to enrich people's lives through music, a mission that he pursued tirelessly until his death.

ments, the reverence of musicians, the fame, the money—they were wonderful, but they didn't affect him as a person. He always insisted that he was just an entertainer, put on earth to make people happy. When that attitude was attacked during the civil rights era as naive and simplistic, he was angry, baffled, and occasionally outspoken.

No matter what else people thought he was, Armstrong remained human—dignified and clowning, complex and simple, full of life's pleasures and sadness. He was often contradictory: he never let anyone dictate how he played his music, but he let his wives and managers run his business affairs. He was generous and openhearted, but he was also fiercely competitive and stubborn.

He lived life as he chose, and that meant hard work and hard play. The music always came first. Once that was taken care of, he loved other pleasures: rich but simple food, cigarettes, an occasional drink, marijuana, the company of women. "Still," as Gary Giddins notes, "he always hit the gig on time and played to the peak of his amazing energy."[4] He insisted on hitting those gigs until old age and illness finally forced him to stop.

Armstrong grew up in poverty, and his early life was rough. That he survived into adulthood is remarkable. That he gave pleasure to others for so many years and with such intensity is amazing. That he also became a world-famous figure who radically changed the course of popular music is simply astonishing.

1 Armstrong's Early Life, 1901-1914

New Orleans, Louisiana, has had a reputation as a wide-open, easygoing city since its founding in the early eighteenth century. A sultry climate created by its location near the mouth of the Mississippi River fosters its laid-back, pleasure-loving atmosphere. Its role as a port city has also made it an important trade center.

The people of New Orleans have always made up a rich cultural stew. Mingled together are descendants of original French settlers, later Spanish and British settlers, slaves and other African Americans from the Caribbean, and others drawn by the city's freewheeling style. By the turn of the century, the city was wild, exciting, and sometimes dangerous. Louis Armstrong was born into this melting pot.

Born on the Fourth of July?

Perhaps the most enduring story about Louis Armstrong is that he was born on the Fourth of July, 1900. It's an appropriate

New Orleans at the turn of the century. A cultural melting pot, the city was known for its laid-back, freewheeling atmosphere.

A Tough Crowd

Louis grew up as a tough kid in the Battlefield neighborhood of New Orleans. In this excerpt from an interview in Jones and Chilton's The Louis Armstrong Story, *he reminisces about those days.*

"I remember running around with a lot of bad boys which did a lot of crazy things. As the saying goes, your environment makes you. My life has always been an open book. There's nothing for me to hide. I have respected everybody as best I could since I was a little shaver. Many a time I would be with kids in my neighborhood and they would play Follow the Leader. So if they would get into any kind of trouble, I would be in trouble also. If they would steal something and get caught, I was in trouble the same as they. Savvy? You must realize it was very shaky all the time during my days in New Orleans. Especially those early ones. They were rough. You had to fight and do a lot of ungodly things to keep from being trampled on. Sure I had fights and did a number of rough things just so I could have a little peace or elbow room as we used to express it.

All boys were bad in those days—you'd better believe it. The kids from the Third Ward were so bad until they carried their pistols on them in holsters like those real cowboys. And you think they won't shoot to kill? Huh! Mayann [Louis's mother] used to tell me, 'Son, don't fight, don't fight.' So I was arguing with a boy one day in school and, thinking of what my mother told me concerning not fighting until you had an excuse, I told this kid, 'OK, since you want to start a fight, hit me.' And he did—right in the eye. Damn near blinded me. But where he made his mistake, he kept standing there to see what I was going to do, while I was feeling for him because I could not see at all. Finally my hand touched him. Yes, you're right, I hung him. I swung on that so-and-so's jaw and head and etc. From that time on I got the name of being a bad boy."

date for someone so closely associated with American music. Louis himself always insisted he was a "firecracker baby." As jazz writer Gary Giddins notes:

That date resounds with a ring of poetic truth for the man who created the music of a new century and doubled as his nation's ambassador of good will. . . . How better to inaugurate an American myth than with a flag-waving birthday?[5]

Unfortunately, it's not true. For many years, no evidence existed to prove or disprove the Fourth of July date for Louis's birth. Record keeping concerning births and deaths among poor black families in the South in those days was casual. Various Armstrong biographers, basing their judgments on sketchy documents, theorize that he was actually born as early as 1898, or as late as 1904.

Not until 1988 was proof found. In the course of researching a biography and video documentary, both called *Satchmo*, Giddins unearthed a baptismal certificate stating that a baby named Louis Armstrong was born to William Armstrong and Mary Albert on August 4, 1901. The baby was baptized three weeks later, on August 25.

This corresponds to another piece of evidence Giddins uncovered. He found a census record for the Battlefield neighborhood of New Orleans dated April 1910. It states that three people lived at 1303 Perdido Street: 23-year-old Thomas Lee, a laborer, Mary Albert, his 25-year-old "companion," and Mary's 8-year-old son, Louis Armstrong.

Louis was, in fact, one year and one month younger than he always claimed. No one knows for certain why he changed the facts of his birth date. As will become clear, however, Louis had some good reasons for lying about his age.

Life in the Battlefield

Louis was probably born on Jane Alley, a small street in the tough New Orleans neighborhood called the Battlefield. (In his autobiography, Armstrong calls the street "James Alley," but photos from the era show street signs marked "Jane.") The

The tough neighborhood where Armstrong grew up, the Battlefield, probably resembled this turn-of-the-century New Orleans slum.

neighborhood was so named because of the fighting that regularly broke out there among its residents.

The Battlefield was about a mile west of Storyville, the famous red-light district of New Orleans. It was a rough area of crowded, poorly built slums. Although the wealthy neighborhoods of New Orleans had many fine examples of French- and Spanish-influenced architecture, much of the city—Jane Alley included—was haphazardly built. As bassist Pops Foster remembers, "New Orleans in those days was a mess. Very few streets had gravel . . . more were just mud."[6]

Louis's mother, Mary Albert, who was known as Mayann, was born in Boutee (pronounced "Boo-tee"), a sugarcane community about seventy miles west of New Orleans. The exact date of her birth is uncertain, but it was probably in the early 1880s. There are no records, but her grandparents had probably been slaves.

Mayann was an erratic caregiver. She would sometimes go off on a drinking spree for days at a time, leaving Louis and

The Myth of Louis's Birth

One of the most enduring stories about Louis is that he was born on the Fourth of July, 1900. It's false, as Gary Giddins conclusively proves in his biography Satchmo. *Still, the story is a good one, and it endures. Giddins writes:*

"Many of us are programmed to recite not only the year Columbus sailed the ocean blue but that of the Battle of Hastings, and we will carry that information to the grave. Only one date in jazz has anything like ecumenical [general] currency: Louis Armstrong's date of birth, July 4, 1900. That date resounds with a ring of poetic truth for the man who created the music of a new century and doubled as his nation's ambassador of good will. From the mid-1930s on it was heavily featured in Armstrong's press packages and articles.

How better to inaugurate an American myth than with a flag-waving birthday? Armstrong insisted his mother called him 'a firecracker baby,' ushered in among Roman candles and a couple of killings in the Battlefield district of New Orleans. Of course, some historians doubted him, citing the ignorance of many poor people when it came to birthdays. They figured the year was correct, but the month and day were chosen later—impoverished blacks in that era often chose July 4 or another holiday. Armstrong enjoyed no annual birthday holidays as a child."

his sister Beatrice in the care of their grandmother Josephine or other relatives. Despite this, however, Mayann was fun-loving and essentially kindhearted. Time and again throughout his life, Louis would remark that she was the one person most responsible for his success.

She worked as a laundress, taking in clothing. Like most blacks in the South in those days, she also did other odd jobs to survive. Louis did not even discount the possibility that she dabbled in prostitution, which was openly tolerated in her neighborhood. In his autobiography, he matter-of-factly writes:

> Whether my mother did any hustling, I cannot say. If she did, she certainly did it out of my sight. One thing is certain: everybody from the church folks to the lowest roughneck treated her with the greatest respect. She was glad to say hello to everybody and she always held her head up.[7]

Louis's father, Willie Armstrong, had a steady job in a turpentine factory. He was a few years older than Mayann, probably born in the mid-1870s. Willie stopped living with Mayann when Louis was born. Mayann had never married him; nor did she wed any of the several "stepfathers" Louis later had (including Thomas Lee, the man mentioned in the 1910 census report).

Louis saw Willie only on rare occasions, such as when Willie marched in the parades for which New Orleans is so famous. Still, Louis writes fondly of him in his autobiography:

> My real dad was a sharp man, tall and handsome and well built. . . . Yes, he was a fine figure of a man, my dad. Or at least that is the way it seemed to me

Louis in 1918 with his mother, Mayann (center), and his sister Beatrice. Louis later credited his mother as responsible for his success.

as a kid when he strutted by like a peacock at the head of the Odd Fellows parade.[8]

Although they didn't live together for any length of time, Mayann and Willie were together on and off in the first years of Louis's life. During one of their periods of reconciliation, another child, Beatrice, was born; she was nicknamed Mama Lucy.

Mayann provided for Louis and Mama Lucy as best she could. Mealtimes, for instance, were uncertain and haphazard. Louis remembered later that some of the best food he had as a child came when one of his "stepfathers," who worked in a restaurant, would bring home the uneaten

Armstrong was heavily influenced by the lively culture of New Orleans, where music was an important part of everyday life. Here, a New Orleans marching band leads a funeral procession in 1910.

portions of leftover meals. Louis's mother would warm these up or give them to him the next day as a picnic lunch.

Music, Music Everywhere

Louis's formal education was as fitful as his eating habits. He did manage to learn to read and write at a school for black children called the Fisk School. His real education took place later, however, as he began soaking up music on the streets of the city.

New Orleans has always been famous for its music. During Louis's childhood, every event was cause for musical celebration to the Creoles, the descendants of Spanish and French settlers who made up the city's elite. The descendants of slaves and Caribbean settlers also brought their own styles. Europeans contributed marches, waltzes, and other forms of music.

Everything had music attached to it, and music could show up anywhere, any-

time. Guitarist Danny Barker, a contemporary of Louis's, recalls, "One of my pleasantest memories as a kid . . . was how a bunch of kids playing, would suddenly hear sounds. It was like a phenomenon, like the Aurora Borealis."[9]

Even funerals had (and still have) music. Traditionally, a New Orleans marching band escorts a casket to the cemetery, playing sad tunes and hymns. It then leads mourners in a parade, often playing happier tunes, to a private home or funeral parlor for a party or wake. Passersby often join in for a few blocks or for the entire procession.

When Louis was growing up, music was so pervasive that even trucks advertising items such as furniture or clothes would use it to attract a crowd. Louis recalls:

The pie man and the waffle man, they all had a little hustle to attract the people. Pie man used to swing something on the bugle and the waffle man ran a big triangle. The junk man had one of them long tin horns they celebrate with at Christmas—could play the blues and everything on it.[10]

Louis often said later that he'd been born with music in his blood and soon developed a keen awareness of it. He once remarked:

Whenever there was a dance or a lawn party the band . . . would stand in front of the place on the sidewalk and play a half hour of good ragtime music [to advertise it]. And us kids would stand or dance on the other side of the street until they went inside.[11]

People in this preelectronic age, especially the poor, made do with their own entertainment. They had no TV, radio, or movies to ease their worries. The best thing about Louis's childhood, without a doubt, was the music of New Orleans. As Louis himself once put it, "I sure had a ball growing up in New Orleans as a kid. We were poor and everything like that, but music . . . kept you rolling."[12]

Deprivation

Louis's childhood was almost unbelievably difficult, and his early deprivations marked him for life. In his biography of Armstrong, Satchmo, *Gary Giddins writes:*

"Some say that Armstrong never had a childhood, others that he never had anything else. All his life he worked hard and played hard. The deprivation of his early years left its mark: After he became an international celebrity, he would astonish other musicians with his genuine gratitude for such amenities as a limousine or posh hospitality. In all his published writings, he remains uncomplaining about those early years. Here is a man who saw life from the gutter up and learned to accept it all. Jane Alley [where Louis was born] was an area so ridden with violence and vice it was known as the Battlefield. For many of his friends, pimps and whores and gamblers and razor-wielding badasses were role models. Armstrong, of course, was different. In order to create music of the spheres you have to be able to hear it, and Armstrong heard it as a siren call leading him out of hell. One has to believe that the generosity-bordering-on-obsession with which he took his music to the masses reflected his own pragmatic confidence in his healing power. Raised in a house of cards in the middle of a gale, he credited music and his mother's love and wisdom with getting him through."

His First Jobs

When he was about eight years old, Louis began singing in a vocal quartet with some friends. They would gather on the street corners of their neighborhood and sing for pennies, which he would share with his mother. Nearly every night, Louis and his friends would take requests from prostitutes and pimps, perfecting their singing style to please the toughest audience. It was an excellent training ground for someone destined to become one of the world's most famous entertainers.

But Louis also held several day jobs during his boyhood. Starting at the age of seven, he began contributing to his family's resources in ways other than music.

Although his autobiography states that his first job was selling newspapers, an unpublished memoir he wrote in 1969 indicates otherwise. It mentions a Jewish family, the Karmofskys, who took him under their wing and gave him a job hauling old junk, such as rags, bones, bottles, and iron. (The family later became promi-

nent merchants in New Orleans.) Louis writes:

> They were always warm and kind to me . . . something a kid could use at seven and just starting out in the world. . . . When I reached the age of eleven, I began to realize that it was the Jewish family who instilled in me singing from the heart.[13]

At various times, Louis also had other ways of making money. One was delivering a type of coal called stone coal. Another was finding old bricks and pounding them into dust. He would sell buckets of this brick dust to prostitutes in his neighborhood. On Saturday nights, the prostitutes mixed the brick dust with urine and scrubbed the steps of their homes to make them shine.

Several biographers have stated that Louis's first instrument was a cornet at the boys' home he would soon enter. According to his unpublished memoir, however, it was actually a tin horn that he played while riding the rag wagon. Then, with help from the Karmofskys, he saved enough to

The intersection near Louis's boyhood home in the Battlefield (pictured) served as an early training ground for the budding musician. At the age of eight Louis began singing with friends on the street corners for pennies.

The Colored Waifs' Home for Boys and its founder, Capt. Joseph Jones (inset). Armstrong received his first real musical training at this home for delinquent youths.

buy his first real instrument—a battered cornet from a pawn shop. He writes: "After blowing into it a while I realize that I could play 'Home Sweet Home'—then here come the blues. From then I was a mess and tootin' away."[14]

To the Waifs' Home

Around 1912, Louis stopped working for the Karmofsky family. The reasons are unclear. It is certain, however, that by this time young Louis had become a hell-raiser.

He was a well-known figure in his neighborhood, and apparently well liked. He had a number of different nicknames, most having to do with his wide, engaging smile: "Dippermouth," "Gatemouth," "Satchelmouth." This last name would later be changed by a British journalist into his most famous nickname: "Satchmo."

But Louis was still a tough kid from a tough neighborhood. It was perhaps inevitable that he would get into trouble. He

had committed no serious crimes, but the authorities had apparently had their eye on him for some time when trouble finally came.

It happened on New Year's Day, 1913. Many people were out celebrating in the streets of New Orleans, shooting off fireworks and even pistols. Accounts vary on the exact events, but it seems that Louis "borrowed" a .38 revolver from one of his "stepfathers," taking it secretly from a trunk. He wanted to shoot it off as part of the festivities.

When another boy fired a pistol across the street, Louis's friends urged him to do the same. Louis pulled out the pistol, fired all six rounds into the air, and almost immediately felt a policeman's hands grip his shoulders.

Louis spent the night in jail and was then ordered to report to the Colored Waifs' Home for Boys—a home for delinquent or orphaned youths. Mayann apparently had little to say in the matter.

The home was an old building in the countryside outside the city. The home's director, a well-respected educator named Capt. Joseph Jones, recalled many years later that Louis had been there briefly twice before. Accounts vary on how long Louis spent there after the incident with the pistol; Louis himself wrote that it was eighteen months, while the home's music director, Peter Davis, says it was five years. The truth is probably somewhere in between.

The Waifs' Home

The home was run along strict military-style regulations. Louis fit in surprisingly well. Perhaps the discipline and rules were what he needed, after what had been, until then, an unregulated and unstructured life. On numerous occasions, Louis later remarked about his disappointment at having to leave the school; apparently it provided a haven that he enjoyed.

But the home's real benefit to Louis was musical. Specifically, it was there that he met Peter Davis, the home's music director. In *Satchmo*, Louis recalls, "Quite naturally I would make a beeline to Mr. Davis and his music. Music has been in my blood since the day I was born."[15]

At first, Louis did not get on well with Davis. The older man did not like the fact

Strength Through Adversity

Louis's hard early years made him into a man who was both tough and submissive, egotistical and humble. In Louis Armstrong: An American Genius, *James Lincoln Collier writes:*

"There was, clearly, a certain amount of contradiction in his character. He was, to use the term everybody tagged him with after he became famous, a 'humble' man—a little bashful, unwilling to offend. And yet this bashful, humble man could walk onto a stage before thousands of people and pour out chorus after chorus of soaring, intense music, audacious as sky rockets, so confident that other musicians scattered before it. The curious thing about Armstrong . . . is that, however shy he may have been, he usually got what he wanted in the end. . . . In circumstances where the strongest men and women were routinely broken, Louis Armstrong could not be defeated. It was, in a way, a miracle that a child with so little going for him should survive so well. . . . Louis Armstrong was a winner. He had 'street smarts,' and in the long run he knew what was best for himself. And this, too, he acquired from growing up in a neighborhood where the hustle was the way of life."

that Louis came from the Battlefield, where only the toughest kids lived. Davis assumed—since Louis had been raised in the company of thieves, prostitutes, and gamblers—that he must also be worthless.

But Louis was a determined young man, and he kept after Davis. Davis finally relented and let him join the home's marching band, which performed in different neighborhoods of the city. He first let him play the tambourine, and then promoted him to the alto horn, then the bugle, and finally, to the cornet.

Davis saw that Louis had talent. He eventually warmed to the young man and encouraged Louis to practice. Sometimes, Davis even took Louis to his own home so that he could play duets with his niece Ida, who played the piano. He helped Louis become a permanent member of the marching band. Louis often talked in later years about how proud he was when the band played in his old neighborhood, because he could show off in front of his friends and neighbors.

Louis was probably released from the home in 1914. His father, Willie, finally wanted to take an active role in his son's life. Willie appealed to the school to release Louis into his custody. Since Willie had a steady job and could care for him, the authorities agreed.

Armstrong played this cornet during his stay at the Colored Waifs' Home. As a member of the home's marching band, Louis enjoyed showing off in front of his friends and neighbors when the band played in his neighborhood.

Louis moved to Willie's home. By now, Willie had a new wife, Gertrude, and children of their own. But Louis did not get along well with his new family. He missed his mother and sister, and soon he was back living with Mayann.

2 A Star in New Orleans, 1914-1922

In the next years, Louis Armstrong evolved from a high-spirited kid with an enthusiasm for music into one of the best musicians in a city bursting at the seams with them. As soon as he left the Waifs' Home, he began steadily playing in cabarets and the rough saloons called honky-tonks. By the time he left New Orleans for Chicago—a move that would set him on the road to international stardom—he was a seasoned pro.

When Armstrong first began playing in the "tonks," jazz had already existed around New Orleans in primitive form for at least ten years. It had evolved from a mingling of musical styles, including black church music and African, French, northern European, and Latin influences.

Pioneers like Bunk Johnson and Buddy Bolden, both trumpet players, were also introducing into it elements of improvisation, which would become one of jazz's most important aspects. So Armstrong didn't invent jazz, as many people believe, although he would soon become its most innovative and important performer.

Armstrong with jazz pioneer Bunk Johnson in 1943. Johnson was one of the first to introduce elements of improvisation, which became an important feature of Armstrong's dynamic jazz style.

Jazz defies exact definition and description. Armstrong himself always made a joke whenever interviewers tried to pin him down on the subject. He'd say, "If you have to ask, Pops, shame on you." Or, "It's all folk music to me—I ain't heard no horses playing it." Or he'd look innocent and say, "Why, it's what I play for a living."

In the early days, the various New Orleans bands played many different styles of music. High-society orchestras played popular songs, waltzes, ragtime, and "serious" concert pieces. Marching bands put the emphasis on military-style brass and percussion instruments.

There were also the bands that played in houses of ill repute and honky-tonks, as well as for picnics and parties. Usually there were three or four pieces in these rough bands, and they always played plenty of the blues. The blues is a style, distinguished by the use of "blue" notes (flatted thirds, fifths, and sevenths), that had developed from African-based folk music in the Mississippi Delta.

White and black musicians played all the various kinds of music, and they shared a sense of community. Pops Foster recalls, "The white and colored musicians around New Orleans all knew each other, and there wasn't any Jim Crow [racial segregation laws] between them. They really didn't much care what color you were."[16] Still, even in the relatively tolerant atmosphere of New Orleans, the races did not mix onstage. It was not until years later that Armstrong would share a stage with musicians of a different race.

Once he was settled at Mayann's, Armstrong began to look for work. His first

New Orleans marching bands emphasized military-style brass and percussion instruments. Like Armstrong, many musicians got their first experience in such bands.

Apprenticeship

One of Louis's most important early experiences as a musician was his riverboat job with Fate Marable's orchestra. It made him a good sight-reader and gave him experience playing every night with seasoned musicians. In Louis Armstrong: An American Genius, *James Lincoln Collier writes:*

"The riverboat jobs over the next three summers [starting in 1919] were an important factor in Armstrong's development as a musician. There comes a time in the life of every young musician when he needs, more than any teacher, a great deal of regular playing to a high standard. Like an athlete, a musician must develop a set of complex conditioned responses, involving minute portions of the muscles, sinews, and nervous system. For the wind player, these are in the main the muscles of the tongue, mouth, cheeks, jaw—indeed, the whole lower face. . . . What is really difficult in brass playing is the embouchure. Movements from note to note on any brass instrument require almost immeasurably small changes in muscle tension in the lips and lower face in general, frequently as often as several times a second. The tongue may strike the back of the teeth at rates ranging up to 500 times a minute. . . . The player obviously cannot think about any of this while it happens. It must be a conditioned response so deeply ingrained that he can instantly produce, with complete confidence, whatever sequence of notes is called for. The only way to acquire this skill is to do it over and over. A young musician has to play tens of millions of notes in millions of combinations before he establishes a solid reliable embouchure. . . . One way or another, Armstrong played those millions of notes and got that sustained chunk of playing time the young player must have. The band played seven nights a week, rehearsed two afternoons a week, and occasionally did other odd jobs, for periods as long as five months at a time. By the time he left the boats in 1921, Louis was an established professional musician and could meet the demands of any ordinary playing job."

paid musical gigs were at saloons like Tom Anderson's and dance palaces like the one known as Funky Butt Hall. He also played occasionally with marching bands like the Tuxedo Brass Band for funerals and other occasions. These jobs paid only about a dollar a night—not enough for a person to live on. Louis had to rely on tips and on day jobs, such as hauling coal, to make ends meet.

The tonks, needless to say, were a rough atmosphere. They were housed in makeshift buildings, and they had colorful names like The Pup, The Cadillac, and Buttsy Fernandez's. Later in his life, Louis loved to tell stories about the characters he knew then, like a gangster called Black Benny.

Black Benny was so tough that he was one of the few African-American men in New Orleans who could go anywhere in the city without fear. Louis always spoke about him with great respect and affection. All his life, Louis was attracted to men with confident, semi-gangsterish airs. The three men who managed him after his career took off, including the one who managed him for most of his life, were such men.

King Oliver

The first band that Armstrong had a major say in was an on-again, off-again affair he put together with Joe Lindsey, a drummer. It must have been good, because it began getting engagements that were turned down by one of the city's top cornetists, Joe "King" Oliver. Oliver had his own band; he also played in Kid Ory's popular orchestra and was a regular member of the Tuxedo Brass Band.

Right from the beginning, King Oliver was Louis's greatest idol. The affection was mutual; Oliver took a liking to the young cornet player and became one of Louis's most important influences, personally as well as professionally. Years later, Louis recalls, "I sure was like a son to him. That's why I call him Papa Joe. . . . He was always my idol. . . . My man Joe—God bless him."[17]

Oliver was a huge man with a huge appetite. For dinner, he might eat an entire roast chicken and several plates full of vegetables and follow it with a whole apple pie, washed down with a dozen cups of coffee. He was also that rarity among musicians, a homebody. Instead of drinking and gambling, Oliver preferred to spend his free time at home with his wife and stepdaughter.

Oliver's wife, Stella, took a liking to Louis, and Louis would often eat meals with the Olivers. "I used to have all my meals at his house, eat just like they did," Louis remarked later. "Big pot of red beans and rice, half-loafs of bread, and a

Cornetist Joe "King" Oliver became one of Armstrong's closest friends.

ham-hock. Drink sugar-water or lemon-ade."[18] All his life, Louis loved such rich, simple food—and all his life, he battled obesity and other health problems related to overeating.

Oliver helped Louis in many ways. One of the most important was to find him his first steady professional engagements, at a pair of clubs called Matranga's and Henry Ponce's. He also arranged for Louis to get a brand new cornet, replacing the beat-up one from the pawn shop.

Armstrong was immensely proud of this horn, but it also proved to be a problem. In his autobiography, he writes:

> I got my first brand-new cornet on the installment plan with "a little bit down" and a "little bit now and then." Whenever my collector would catch up with me and start talking about a "little bit now" I would tell him, "I'll give you-all a little bit then, but I'm damned if I can give you-all a little bit now."[19]

Kid Ory

In November 1917, the city's famous red-light district, Storyville, was closed by the U.S. Navy. Apparently, this was because too many sailors were getting in trouble there. Louis recalled, "Some sailors on leave got mixed up in a fight and two of them were killed. The Navy started a war on Storyville, and even as a boy I could see that the end was near."[20]

By the fall of 1918, Armstrong felt confident enough to quit his job hauling coal. Besides, when the war ended he had no longer needed a steady paycheck to avoid the draft. On Armistice Day (now called Veterans Day), he simply walked away

from his mule-drawn wagon, thinking to himself, "The war is over. And here I am monkeyin' around with this mule. Huh!"[21]

The closure of Storyville resulted in a tremendous loss of work for musicians in New Orleans. Many, including King Oliver, began to look for work elsewhere. Early in 1919, Oliver left for Chicago. Oliver's departure was a turning point for his protégé.

Louis had just seen Oliver off on the train and was on his way back to his coal cart when Kid Ory found him. Ory was the trombonist who led the top band Oliver regularly played with. Louis later wrote:

> "He [Kid Ory] said that when the boys in the band found out for sure that Joe Oliver was leaving, they told him to go get Little Louis to take Joe's

Trombonist Kid Ory invited Armstrong to become a member of his popular orchestra in 1919.

Meeting Two Musicians

On the riverboat, Louis encountered two other young musicians, cornetist Bix Beiderbecke and trombonist Jack Teagarden, who would become important later in his life. In a Life *magazine interview reprinted as* Louis Armstrong—A Self-Portrait, *he remembers:*

"Each spring we used to go to Davenport, Iowa, where they kept the boats in chutes all winter. That's where I first met Bix Beiderbecke. That was his home. At the time he was just a nice ofay [white] kid the young musicians wanted to introduce to me. Never heard him play until I got his record. . . . Later on in Chicago when I was playing the Sunset Cafe, he'd make a beeline for there when he finished playing at the Chicago theater with Paul Whiteman. At 4 o'clock after the doors were closed, we'd all sit around and play a couple of hours. I was thrilled to death with whatever Bix did. He and I never had no contests. He knocked me out. He had such beautiful tone, those beautiful phrases, fingers fast. Yeah, he was my man. Choice man, too. Quiet. Never satisfied with his solos, and people raving. Always figured he had one better. . . .

[Another time] we'd just put into New Orleans and on the levee was a cat named Jack Teagarden wanting to meet me—but I'd never heard of him. And then when he joined my band years later, it was like a holiday—we understood each other so wonderful. There ain't going to be another Jack Teagarden. . . . He was from Texas, but it was always, 'You a spade [black man], and I'm an ofay [white man]. We got the same soul. Let's blow'—and that's the way it was. He kept all his sad moments, his grievances, to himself. But I could tell his whole heart, his life coming out of that horn. And it was all good."

place. He was a little in doubt at first, but after he'd looked around the town he decided I was the right one to have a try at taking that great man's place. So he told me to go wash up and then come play a gig with them the very same night.[22]

Daisy

Only a few weeks after the armistice, Louis entered into the first of his four marriages. The woman was Daisy Parker, a Creole prostitute from the small town of

Gretna. "We were both young and giddy," Louis later wrote in his memoirs. "She was a little skinny, but she was cute."[23]

Daisy was twenty-one at the time, and Louis was eighteen. Mayann gave the marriage her blessing. She felt that Louis was his own man, and, despite comments made by neighbors about her son's choice, felt that he should make up his own mind.

The young couple found an apartment of their own, but the marriage was not a match made in heaven. They began fighting and even went to jail occasionally because of their public spats. Daisy was hotheaded, jealous, and fond of using a razor to make her feelings clear—she once sliced up Louis's expensive new hat out of spite. He recalls that, after the wedding,

> I found out she couldn't even read or write. All she knew how to do was fuss and fight. But it's a funny thing about two people being in love—whatever little traits there are, no matter how unpleasant they may be, love will drown them out.[24]

Louis and Daisy separated shortly after the wedding. However, they continued to see each other occasionally until 1922, when Louis left town for good.

One family commitment that began for Louis during this time, however, would continue for many years. Louis and Daisy were baby-sitting Clarence Armstrong, the infant son of Louis's cousin, Flora Miles, when Clarence accidentally fell off their balcony during a rainstorm. He suffered permanent brain damage. Although Louis never legally adopted Clarence, he took financial responsibility for him after that and continued to do so for the rest of his life.

Armstrong (second from left) assumed financial responsibility for his cousin Clarence (far right) after the boy was injured while in the care of the musician.

On the Cruise Ships

In the summer of 1919, Armstrong took another step forward in his professional progress. A prominent musician named Fate Marable heard him playing with Kid Ory. Marable worked on a pleasure riverboat that cruised up and down the Mississippi. He played the calliope to attract people onshore and led a dance band on board. As soon as he heard Louis play, Marable hired him for the band.

It was an invaluable experience for Louis. For three summers in a row, he was able to play in a top band that performed several shows a night, seven nights a week. He was forced to perform at the peak of his ability, in the presence of musicians who constantly challenged him to do his best.

He also learned to read music well, which had been a weak point for him. As he remarks:

> Of course I could pick up a tune fast, for my ears were trained . . . but not enough for Fate Marable's band. Fate knew all this when he hired me, but he liked my tone and the way I could catch on. . . . He knew that just by being around musicians who read music I would automatically learn myself.[25]

The riverboat job may explain the controversy regarding Louis's true age and birth date. He apparently lied about his age when he registered for the draft in 1918, telling the draft board that he was a year older than he really was. It is likely that he did this to make it seem that he was not a minor.

If the authorities had known he was only eighteen, he could not legally have played clubs in upriver states where the riverboat stopped. As biographer Giddins notes:

> The false birthdate allowed him to embark on a career he was impatient to pursue. When the wily manager Joe Glaser took charge of his career [many years later], the date passed into legend.[26]

A Message Arrives

Up to this point, Louis had resisted all offers to leave the city. In fact, with the

Armstrong (third from right) gained valuable experience during his three-summer stint in Fate Marable's orchestra, which played aboard a pleasure boat on the Mississippi River.

A publicity photo of King Oliver's Creole Jazz Band. Armstrong jumped at the chance to play in Oliver's band, which was making a name for itself in Chicago.

exception of the riverboat excursions, which took him up the Mississippi, Louis had never been outside New Orleans and had rarely set foot outside his familiar neighborhoods.

But in August 1922, a telegram arrived that was to change Louis's mind. It was from King Oliver, asking Louis to come to Chicago and join his Creole Jazz Band, which was enjoying considerable success there.

Oliver was still Louis's idol and mentor. Armstrong wouldn't have dreamed of turning down the proposal, even though it meant playing second cornet to Oliver's lead.

On August 8, he caught an evening train for Chicago. He took little more than his cornet, a few changes of clothes, and (because black people traveling by train in those days could eat only what they packed with them) a fish sandwich prepared by Mayann. It was the start of a journey that would take him to places he had never even dreamed about.

3 The Beginnings of Fame, 1922-1925

The mid-1920s marked the beginnings of stardom for Armstrong. His brilliant appearances with King Oliver's band in Chicago caused a sensation and brought him a measure of fame and money. The new medium of radio helped spread his name beyond the city as his live broadcasts and early recordings were heard by admirers around the country.

Louis Arrives

Joe Oliver was supposed to meet Louis at the train station. But the train was late, and by the time it arrived Oliver had already left for his nightly engagement at the Lincoln Gardens cabaret. Fortunately, Oliver had alerted a station employee, who made sure that Louis was put in a taxi to Lincoln Gardens.

Lincoln Gardens was one of the largest and most popular dance nightclubs in Chicago. It was not a "black and tan" club—that is, one catering to a mixed-race audience—but it often had white patrons along with its regular black clientele. It could pack one thousand jazz fans in at a time to hear the exciting new music. James Lincoln Collier notes that it "is probably the most celebrated band lo-

cation in jazz history, for it was here that the Northern musicians and the early jazz fans of both races began to acquire the true faith."[27]

Louis was frightened when he walked into the club that evening. The band he heard on the stand was so good that he feared he was out of his league. But Oliver

By the mid-1920s when this photo was taken, Armstrong was well on his way toward musical stardom.

welcomed him warmly and invited him to just sit and listen.

Armstrong rehearsed with the band the next afternoon, and that night made his debut. It didn't take him long to fit in. He later remarked that "I was all ears, sittin' up there listenin' and figurin' to myself, and almost before I could turn around Joe Oliver and me was playing duets and crackin' out trumpet breaks together."[28] (Although Armstrong used the word "trumpet" in this recollection, in fact he would not start using the trumpet regularly in addition to the cornet for a few more years.)

Oliver and his protégé quickly worked out a system of playing that depended largely on intuition and rapport. Oliver always took the lead, and Louis would watch him carefully to see how he could follow and fill in. Essentially, Oliver's cornet was the band's lead voice, with the rest of the band supplying backup and Armstrong echoing the leader's solo passages, which are called breaks.

It was strictly a supporting role, but Louis was delighted to be there, sharing the stage with his idol. As trombonist Preston Jackson puts it:

When you saw Joe lean over towards Louis at the first ending, you would know they were going to make a break in the middle of the next chorus. And what breaks they made! Louis never knew what Joe was going to play, but he would always follow him perfectly.[29]

Their rapport soon became the talk of the town. Chicagoans had never heard anything like it. Armstrong recalls:

All the white cats from downtown. . . . would come by after their work and sit up by the band and listen until the place shut. They didn't understand how we did it, without [sheet] music or anything. . . . Couldn't nobody

The musical rapport between Armstrong (kneeling) and Oliver (standing, center) earned the Creole Jazz Band a strong following. While Oliver took the lead, Armstrong followed the musical passages perfectly.

Fame

Louis loved becoming famous in Chicago, but it had its disadvantages too. He was always afraid that being a celebrity would alienate him from people. In an interview in the April 15, 1966, issue of Life *magazine, he remarks:*

"See, I never did want to be a big mucky-muck star. At the Vendome they said, 'You're going over so big, you get up on the stage to play your solos [instead of being in the pit with the rest of the band] and we'll give you more money.' I thought it was stupid and I wouldn't do it. They said, 'Look at what it'll mean to you.' I didn't see what it'd mean. Finally they just put a light on me in the pit. If I'd gotten up there on that stage, people would say, 'Shoot, he just wants to be a star, an individual,' and even your own musicians you're playing with, you won't get the same warmth. See, I tried to have fun as long as I could, but they wouldn't keep it that way.

You know you don't have no fun at all if you get too famous. I mean, for a lot of years now, I don't have but a few nights off, and I can't go no place they don't roll up the drum, you have to stand up and take a bow, get up on the stage. And sitting in an audience, I'm signing programs for hours all through the show. And you got to sign them to be in good faith. And afterwards all those hangers-on get you crowded in at the table—and you *know* you're going to pay for the check."

trick us; the musicians thought we were marvelous.[30]

The idea of using two cornets (or trumpets) as lead instruments was not a new one, but Oliver and Armstrong gave it a stamp of their own by communicating personal warmth through their solos. As Max Jones and John Chilton write, this was essential. "Every performance of classic New Orleans jazz depends on the personality of each player as well as on his willingness to submerge some of his individuality for the good of the ensemble."[31]

That Toddlin' Town

Once he settled in with the band and saw it would work, Armstrong realized that Chicago would be home for a while. It was very different from the world he had known. Far from being the easy-going, warm-weather, ramshackle city of his youth, Chicago was a tough, brash go-getter of a city.

Armstrong's immediate environment was dominated by an especially rough breed: the Chicago gangster. As James Lincoln Collier puts it:

By bringing the New Orleans jazz sound to Chicago, the Original Dixieland Jazz Band paved the way for Armstrong and others to enjoy fame in Chicago.

In New Orleans music was for fun; in Chicago it was an adjunct of a vast, gang-dominated entertainment industry, and, as such, its function was to make money. The one characteristic that Chicago held in common with New Orleans was the rich variousness of its vice.[32]

Professional criminals controlled vast areas of the city's trade. They had their own lawyers, doctors, and even hospitals, where they could be treated with no questions asked. They also supplied the liquor to and were hidden partners in many, if not most, of Chicago's clubs and cabarets. Armstrong, whether he liked it or not, was in the center of this world.

There is no evidence that he was in any way actively involved with the mobs.

The managers he acquired in Chicago, however, had some unsavory gangland connections, and it is possible that gang influence or money was sometimes used to help Armstrong's career.

On the other hand, Chicago was primed for jazz, and this was to Armstrong's advantage. One of the first groups to have brought the new sound of jazz out of New Orleans was a derivative but influential all-white group called the Original Dixieland Jazz Band that had paved the way in Chicago in 1917.

The closing of Storyville sped up the process, sending many New Orleans natives northward. The sizable black community in Chicago was thus receptive to jazz (as was the smaller group of white fans). According to musicologist Arnold

Shaw, "By 1920 there were so many jazzmen in Chicago, most of them black, that the center of jazz had shifted."[33]

The First Recordings

An important step Louis took around this time was into the recording studio. In April 1923, King Oliver's Creole Jazz Band recorded nine tracks for the Gennett Company in Richmond, Indiana. These were Armstrong's first appearances on record.

The titles included "Canal Street Blues," "Dippermouth Blues," and "Chimes Blues," the latter featuring Louis's first recorded solo. The musicians generally got fifty dollars each for a session, recording two or four "sides" (tunes) per session.

The recording industry was in its infancy in the 1920s. Musicians played together into large bell-shaped horns, and the resulting vibrations were recorded by carving directly onto wax platters or cylinders. The use of separate microphones and dubbing were years in the future.

Armstrong had such huge tone and wind power that the Gennett engineers made him stand over in one corner of the studio, away from the recording horn, lest he overpower the band. Pianist Lil Hardin later recalled:

> Joe and Louis stood right next to each other as they always had, and you couldn't hear a note that Joe was playing. . . . So . . . they put Louis about fifteen feet over in the corner, looking all sad. . . . He thought it was bad for him to have to be separated from the band. I looked at him and smiled to reassure him that he was all right.[34]

Between April and December, Oliver's band made a total of thirty-seven recordings for Gennett as well as for three other companies: OKeh, Columbia, and Paramount. They did other recordings as well,

Early recording methods were primitive by today's standards. Musicians played together into a large horn. Their notes activated a vibrating needle that etched markings onto a wax cylinder that was pressed against a vinyl disk to create a record.

New York in the Twenties

"The dance boom was going strong. Prohibition had been in operation for four years and going out to get drunk in illegal speakeasies had become invested with glamour. The new hot music was very much in vogue. For young people, the thing to do was to go out to the cabarets to drink and dance to jazz. Catering to them were some 2500 speakeasies, cabarets, and restaurants selling illegal liquor in midtown Manhattan alone. Many of these clubs and restaurants featured music. The best-known were in the so-called Broadway area around Times Square and in Harlem around Lenox and Seventh Avenue for several blocks on either side of 135th St. 'Jazz and night clubs have been synonymous from the beginning,' the NY *Times* reported in 1930.

As important as the nightclubs in providing a base for musicians were the dance halls. They required continuous music, which usually meant hiring two bands. There were, according to a New York City citizens' commission, which was concerned about the immorality of 'slow jazz, which tempo in itself is the cause of most of the sensual and freakish dancing,' 238 dance halls in Manhattan, grossing five million dollars annually. According to the commission, these dance halls provoked 'much immorality and drinking,' but from the perspective of jazz they were exceedingly important in supporting hundreds of musicians and in providing places where the new hot music could develop."

but these have been lost. Oliver's early recordings still stressed polyphony with everyone playing together in classic New Orleans style. In other words, there were as yet no real solos.

Still, these records were important milestones in jazz. As the early jazz critic Hughes Panassié writes in *The Real Jazz*:

The extraordinary thing about these interpretations is the perfect equilibrium which the musicians achieve in improvisation, and the grace and melodic clarity which reigns from the beginning to the end.[35]

One of them, "Heebie Jeebies," became a commercial hit. It sold forty thousand copies in the space of a few weeks—this in a market where five thousand copies sold was considered respectable.

Miss Lil

Soon after his arrival, it became clear that Armstrong was a serious rival to Oliver for the title of Chicago's top jazz player. In fact, Louis's superior talent would soon break the two apart. Before that happened though, another person began to have a strong influence on Louis.

Lil Hardin was a classically trained piano player from a middle-class home in Memphis, Tennessee. She had been class valedictorian at Fisk University. Instead of following her classical training, however, she fell under the spell of jazz. She eventually joined King Oliver's Chicago band and became one of the few women to make waves in early jazz as an instrumentalist, not a singer.

Lil was good-looking, smart, and talented, and it seems that every man in the band had his eye on her. Louis once remarked, "From the first night on the bandstand I noticed that all the boys in Joe's band had been very busy trying to make a play for Lil, who was the Belle of the Windy City of Chicago at that time."[36]

Lil was not thrilled by the kid from down south when they first met. She later reminisced:

> I'd been hearing from all the musicians about him—Little Louis they'd called him—and what a good player he was. So they brought him in and "Little Louis" was all of 226 pounds! . . . I didn't like the way he was dressed; I didn't like the way he talked; and I just didn't like him.[37]

But she soon began paying attention to his talent. Oliver confessed to her that "this Louis, he's a better trumpet player than I'll ever be. . . . As long as I keep him playing second to me he won't get ahead of me. I'll still be the king."[38] After that, she began to look beyond the funny clothes and country-bumpkin accent, concentrating instead on his playing.

Her focus soon turned from the musical to the personal. The change, however, was not immediately noticeable to Armstrong. He once said, "I was so wrapped up in music and did not pay any attention at first to the fact that Lil was stuck on me. . . . 'Who me?' I thought to myself."[39]

Eventually Louis caught on, however, and the two began going out together. After Mayann visited Chicago and told Louis she approved of Lil, he filed for a divorce from Daisy Parker. Lil, meanwhile, divorced

Despite her initial impression that the young musician was a "country bumpkin," pianist Lil Hardin eventually fell in love with and married Louis Armstrong.

New York Experience

Louis would not become a major star during his first stay in New York. That would have to wait until his next trip there. But he did have an impact on musicians and jazz fans there. In their biography of Armstrong, Max Jones and John Chilton write:

"In this first New York stay Armstrong scored a success only with musicians and those dancers and music fans who bothered to note who was playing what. He commented once that five years after his visit Broadway finally accepted him. The experience, however, had been vastly worthwhile for him professionally. In the year with Henderson he gained confidence, improved his knowledge of reading and interpreting a score, learned many new tricks of showmanship, and picked up ideas from dozens of musicians he heard and, in some cases, recorded with.

New York was the last of Louis' universities. There were still finer points of the music game to be mastered, and he was as eager as ever to learn them, but he returned to Chicago a marvelous and mature all-round musician."

her estranged husband, an aspiring singer. On February 5, 1924, Louis and Lil were married at Chicago City Hall.

Leaving Mr. Joe

Lil was constantly urging Louis to better himself. She made him improve his sight-reading and suggested that he would be better off as a solo act. She once said:

I thought the best thing to do was to get him away from Joe. I encouraged him to develop himself, which was all he needed. He's a fellow who didn't have much confidence in himself to begin with.[40]

Louis began deferring to his new wife on almost everything. Since they worked in the same band, this did not go unnoticed. Louis took a lot of ribbing from other men, and some of the band members began calling him "Henny"—as in hen-pecked.

He seems not to have minded it terribly. He later said that the ones doing the teasing were always broke, while he always had money. In fact, he seems to have appreciated having a strong figure like Lil to make decisions for him. He once said:

If she did engineer my life, she had a perfect right to. We were married, and heard the preacher when he said to love, honor and obey. And to me that's what was happening.[41]

Still, Louis was reluctant to leave Oliver's band. He was comfortable there—content to stay in the shadow of his beloved mentor. But Lil finally convinced him to give notice. She did it by making an ultimatum: "Leave Mr. Joe," she said, "or leave me."

Louis couldn't bring himself to tell Oliver himself, and he asked another band member, saxophonist Rudy Jackson, to do it. Oliver took the news quietly. Jackson later recalled that Oliver said at the time that he knew Louis was the better player, and that he (Oliver) was lucky that Louis had stayed with him as long as he had.

Oliver's story later on is a sad one. He contracted a gum disease that made playing painful, had difficulty keeping bands together, and drifted into obscurity. Armstrong periodically sent money to his old friend and teacher in later years. In 1937, Armstrong found Oliver running a vegetable stand in Georgia. King Oliver died soon after of a cerebral hemorrhage.

On His Own

Louis officially left Oliver's band at the end of June 1924. Lil had already lined up a job for him in a band at the Dreamland Cafe. Armstrong did well in this solo spot. As he later remarked:

> I listened very carefully when Lil told me I should play first cornet. "Play second to no one," she said. "They don't get great enough." She proved she was right, didn't she? [42]

In September, Armstrong got another telegram that would change his life. It was from Fletcher Henderson, a New York bandleader and piano player. Henderson had heard Armstrong years before in New Orleans and had tried to get him to come to New York then.

Henderson's band was extremely successful—the highest ranking black band in the country. Henderson knew that Louis would fit in well. He later recalled:

> Knowing the way that horn sounded, I had to try to get him for my band. . . . Truthfully, I didn't expect him to accept the offer and I was very surprised when he came to New York and joined us. [43]

The offer was for fifty-five dollars a week. This was less money than Armstrong was used to making, but it was also a chance at the big time. He was a star in Chicago but not well known outside the city. Lil convinced him to accept the offer.

Bandleader Fletcher Henderson was pleasantly surprised when Armstrong agreed to come to New York to play in his top-ranking band.

A band plays to a packed house at the Savoy in Harlem in the 1920s. Dance halls and cabarets had become a booming business, creating great demand for popular bands like Henderson's.

The Big Apple

Musical tastes were changing in the mid-twenties, and Armstrong changed with them. The demand for small-band "hot" jazz had decreased. Silent movies had swept the land, creating a need for large, sweeter orchestras that could accompany them. These bands were also popular in dance halls, and it was in one of New York's finest—Roseland—that Henderson's band held court.

New York was then, as it still is, a mecca for any serious musician. The dance-hall and cabaret business was booming. Prohibition had been in force for several years, and going to speakeasies was the glamorous thing to do. These clubs supported thousands of musicians, even if they were playing tightly arranged dance music and not improvised jazz.

Henderson wanted to augment his normal lineup—two trumpets, two saxophones, one trombone, plus banjo, piano, drums, and tuba—with a third trumpet. Armstrong would therefore not be in a lead position, but would be used as a kind of specialist—as the kid who could play hot jazz choruses on demand within the band context.

Louis still looked the part of a country bumpkin. Drummer Kaiser Marshall remembers that Armstrong showed up for rehearsal in big, thick-soled boots that clumped on the floor. The New York sophisticates weren't sure what to make of the new kid, but as soon as he played there was little doubt. As Gary Giddins puts it:

The spell Armstrong cast on the best musicians in New York can hardly be overestimated. Only one other soloist in jazz history, Charlie Parker, in the 1940s, would ever cast so wide a net over every breed of musician.[44]

Although Henderson's band has been criticized by some jazz fans for its sweet sound, it had a number of strong points. Among its members were saxophonists Buster Bailey and Coleman Hawkins, who would both become important in the history of jazz, as well as a gifted arranger, Don Redman. Louis quickly established himself as worthy of this company. As Bailey puts it:

> Louis had the same impact in New York that he had made in Chicago when he first came there. He always made the greatest impression on musicians when they heard him.[45]

Still, that impact was mainly felt within the relatively small world of musicians and fans. It would be several years before a wider audience would become aware of him.

The band spent six months at Roseland, and recorded often during that period. These were Louis's first recordings since leaving Oliver, although he had no chance to solo on them. The band then toured New England—the first black band to do so—and spent the summer playing a hall in Lawrence, Massachusetts.

On His Own Again

Henderson appreciated some of what Armstrong could do, but "the kid" felt frustrated. After fourteen months and forty records, Armstrong left the band, fed

As a member of Henderson's band Armstrong was surrounded by exceptional talent. The band's members included saxophonist Coleman Hawkins (left), who would leave his own mark on the history of jazz, and gifted arranger Don Redman (right).

After fourteen months of playing with Henderson's orchestra, Armstrong (top row, center) left the band to venture out on his own. He had become frustrated with not being allowed solo space or an opportunity to sing.

up with not being allowed solo space or an opportunity to sing.

This latter objection was especially frustrating. Armstrong had been singing in public since he was a boy. He loved it and knew that it went over well with audiences. But Henderson had his doubts. Many years later, Henderson told an interviewer:

> About three weeks after he joined us, [Louis] asked me if he could sing a number. I know I wondered what he could possibly do with that big fish horn voice of his, but finally I told him to try it. He was great. The band loved it, and the crowd just ate it up.[46]

Still, Henderson did not provide enough solo space to satisfy Louis. There was also pressure from Lil to return to Chicago—especially after she got word that Louis's eye had been caught by more than one woman in New York. Lil lined up a job for him in the Windy City to entice him back.

Louis's time with the Henderson band was extremely worthwhile professionally. He gained confidence, continued to improve his sight-reading, and learned new tricks of showmanship. As Max Jones and John Chilton put it:

> New York was the last of Louis' universities. There were still finer points of the music game to be mastered, and he was as eager as ever to learn them, but he returned to Chicago a marvelous and mature all-round musician.[47]

Chapter

4 Return to Chicago, 1925-1929

When Armstrong returned to Chicago in late 1925, it was with star billing. His sojourn in New York had solidified his reputation, and he was a guaranteed draw. The band he played with at the Dreamland Cafe was Lil's in name, but everyone knew who the star was.

Armstrong's workaholic habits were satisfied with several gigs a day and a busy recording schedule. And the records he made during this period—the Hot Five and Hot Seven sides—are classics, regard-

ed by many as the purest things he ever recorded.

Still, there were some hard times during this second extended stay in Chicago. Armstrong tried opening his own club—with disastrous results. His marriage to Lil was shaky. By the end of the decade, he was broke, out of work, and on his way back to New York.

Soon after he started the Dreamland job, Armstrong also got a gig with Erskine Tate's orchestra. This was a big band that

Armstrong's brief stint with Erskine Tate's orchestra gave him the opportunity to sing and to showcase his talent with exciting solos.

Return to Gangland Chicago

When Louis returned to Chicago in 1925, it was an even wilder place than when he left. In his biography of Armstrong, James Lincoln Collier writes that an estimated ten thousand professional criminals were operating in the city at the time.

"The gangsters had their own lawyers, doctors, bondsmen, fences, and even hospitals, where they could go for repairs with no questions and no reports to the police. . . . The extent to which the entertainment business in Chicago was run by the gangs cannot be overestimated, they supplied the liquor and were hidden partners in many, if not most, clubs and cabarets in the city. A lot of them were heavy drinkers, and they not only owned the clubs but frequented them. Many stories have been told of gangsters coming into clubs they owned, locking the place, and ordering the band to play a favorite number over and over all night long. . . . Armstrong, thus, worked in an atmosphere saturated with gangsters. . . . A headliner, such as Armstrong was about to become, could not simply change jobs as it suited him if the gangsters objected. Armstrong was almost certainly not actively involved with the mobs, and it does not appear that he was ever directly controlled by the gangs . . . but some of his later managers had gangland connections, and it is probable that at times gang influence or money was necessary to smooth Armstrong's professional way."

played for movies at the Vendome Theater. The orchestra also performed between shows.

Louis had a different featured number each week and was able to solo fairly often within the band context. His specialty was hitting difficult high notes endlessly, which drove crowds wild with excitement. "I was at home then," he said later. "That's when I could hit 50 high C's and more, maybe pick up a megaphone and sing a few choruses of 'Heebie Jeebies' or sump'n. . . . It was beautiful."[48]

Early in 1926, Louis left Dreamland and found a new job, with Carroll Dickerson's band at the Sunset Cafe. He was then shuttling madly between two jobs—playing four shows at the Vendome starting at seven, then racing off at eleven to play at the Sunset until three or four in the morning. The schedule was exhausting, but the constant exposure forced Armstrong to perfect his stage presence.

The Sunset was a "black and tan"—a mixed-race club—although it was located in a predominantly black neighborhood.

It featured big production numbers with lots of chorus girls and other trappings. At the Sunset, Armstrong really launched his career as a general entertainer. By the end of his stay there, his singing and joking was as much a part of his act as playing the trumpet.

Hines and Glaser

At the Sunset, Armstrong met two important people. One was Earl "Fatha" Hines, the Dickerson band's gifted pianist. At the time, Hines was the only musician in Chicago who could approach Armstrong as a musical equal. The two of them hit it off personally, and it was the beginning of a long and fruitful collaboration.

The other person was Joe Glaser, whose mother owned the building housing the Sunset. Glaser may have managed the club for a period. He would later be-come Louis's manager and confidante, a position he held until his death many years later.

Dickerson, the bandleader at the Sunset, had a serious drinking problem, and eventually was fired. Early in 1927, Louis replaced him, and the group was renamed Louis Armstrong and His Stompers. This was the first time Louis had led a band under his own name at a major club.

Hines became the band's musical director. This marked the start of a lifelong habit for Armstrong. He found he preferred to have another person at the helm of his bands. This gave him the freedom to concentrate on playing, leaving such responsibilities as hiring and firing to the director.

During his tenure at the Sunset, Armstrong began using the trumpet more than the cornet, and eventually he stopped using the cornet entirely. The main difference between the two instruments is in tone. The trumpet is louder,

Pianist Earl "Fatha" Hines and Armstrong enjoyed a long and fruitful collaboration after Hines became musical director of Armstrong's band, Louis Armstrong and His Stompers.

Louis Armstrong and His Stompers at the Sunset Cafe in 1927. With his new band, Armstrong made the transition from the cornet to the louder, less mellow-sounding trumpet.

but it has a less mellow tone. The cornet had been more popular with New Orleans bands, but Armstrong found that the trumpet went over more successfully with the larger bands in which he now played.

Home Life Falters

Louis liked the Sunset because of the musicians, including Fatha Hines. The money was also good. But another reason Louis switched from the Dreamland job to the one at the Sunset is that he wanted to avoid Lil, the Dreamland bandleader.

Louis and Lil were both working and making good money at the time—about seventy-five dollars a week each. They'd acquired several things, including a house, a car, and some vacation land. Lil was still "managing" Louis, helping him read the difficult charts used in Tate's orchestra and vetoing his idea of rejoining King Oliver at one point. But on a personal level they were not getting along well.

Louis began seeing Lil only on and off. He began to keep company instead with Alpha Smith, who worked as a maid for a wealthy white family. Alpha was a

beauty who had no trouble helping Louis spend his earnings. He remembered later:

> Wow, was I making nice money, so I had a good chance to buy Alpha some nice things with my extra money Lil didn't know about. . . . I used to take her out on Sunday and we would drive out to Blue Island . . . in my brand new Ford car with the yellow wire wheels.[49]

With his marriage to Lil on the rocks, Armstrong began seeing Alpha Smith (pictured). The couple married in 1938.

Making Records

The first records Louis made were done on primitive recording equipment. Musicians blew directly into a large acoustic horn and the results were cut directly onto wax recordings. In an interview in the April 15, 1966, issue of Life *magazine, Louis recalls:*

"But you better just enjoy yourself with those records, because you'll never know how those cats really did sound. Joe Oliver's best days are not on record. They were in New Orleans—in fact I think he blew himself out in those street parades. And making these records, everybody tense, and we'd all played into one big horn, like the one on His Master's Voice. There weren't no mikes. And my tone was so much stronger than Joe Oliver's that when we recorded for Gennett I had to stand way over by the door so I wouldn't overshadow him. The only way you could put your solo in was to run over to that horn. Couldn't have a drum because it would make the needle jump off the wax—and how you going to play without a drummer? Keeps that tempo and that rhythm and that feeling."

The Usonia and the Savoy

In the spring and summer of 1927, Armstrong's career took a bad turn. In April, he quit the Vendome Theater for another, the Metropolitan, because the pay was better. In July, the Sunset Cafe closed and Louis went to the Black Hawk, a major club that catered mainly to white audiences.

When that job ended, Armstrong started scuffling. He teamed up with Hines and drummer Zutty Singleton, an old friend from New Orleans who had been in the Dickerson band. The three vowed to look for jobs together and not to work if the others couldn't. Louis remembered later:

> Things [got] so tough with us until fifteen cents looked like fifteen dollars. But we did not lose our spirit, and we all kept that ol' clean shirt on every-

day, and ol' Earl Hines kept the big fresh cigar in his mouth everyday.[50]

Eventually, the three pooled their resources and opened their own club: the

For a short time Armstrong's band headlined at the Black Hawk, a club that catered mostly to white audiences.

Usonia in the Warwick Hall on 47th Street. But when a large, well-funded club, the Savoy, opened only two blocks away, it pulled the Usonia's audience away. The new venture died before it really had a chance.

Shortly after the Usonia closed, Louis found work again—ironically, at the club that had forced his own to close. Carroll Dickerson, Louis's boss from the Sunset, had been hired to lead the band at the Savoy. He asked Louis and Zutty Singleton to join it.

Unfortunately, Hines was temporarily out of town when the offer came. Instead of waiting for him, as the three had promised each other they'd do, Armstrong and Singleton accepted. Hines was furious when he found out and refused to join the band even when formally asked. He would work with Armstrong again many years later, but the bitter feelings never went entirely away.

Not everyone else felt entirely warm feelings towards Louis. One of these was Dave Peyton, a respected musician and an elder statesman in Chicago's black community. Peyton used his weekly newspaper column to urge musicians to upgrade the image of African Americans. Peyton loved Armstrong and praised him often, but didn't care for the raucous music he was now playing. "This orchestra of Louis' . . . is noisy, corrupt, contemptible, and displeasing to the ear. . . . Louis will learn in time to come that noise isn't music."[51]

The Classic Recordings

Peyton's criticisms notwithstanding, during this period Armstrong made some of the most famous music in all of jazz. In these records, the first under his own name, he pioneered a crucial concept in jazz—the improvised solo. They are glorious examples of a natural genius at the peak of his creative powers.

Collectively, they are known as the Hot Five and Hot Seven records. They were made between 1925 and 1928—a total of 65 performances for the OKeh Recording Company. Their importance cannot be overestimated.

If he had stopped performing after making them, Louis would never have become an international star, a goodwill ambassador, or a beloved folk hero. But, Gary Giddins writes:

> He would still be regarded as the single most creative and innovative force in jazz history. Notwithstanding a handful of trite numbers and the intrusion of some vaudeville hokum, the OKeh recordings are no more dated— which is to say, diminished in the power to enlighten and astonish—than Bach cantatas.[52]

The band Armstrong assembled for these recordings was strictly a studio band. It never performed in public. Besides the leader, it consisted of Lil on piano, banjo player Johnny St. Cyr, clarinetist Johnny Dodds, and trombonist Kid Ory. With the occasional addition of tuba player Pete Briggs and drummer Baby Dodds, the band became the Hot Seven.

Even with the crude recording techniques used then, the obvious joy Louis took in playing shines clearly through these records. He was happy to be among musicians he knew and liked, playing music which he'd helped evolve from the collective improvisation pioneered by his hero, Joe Oliver.

Louis Armstrong and his Hot Five (left) and Hot Seven bands were strictly studio bands that assembled for recordings by the OKeh Recording Company (below). These records were the first to exploit Armstrong's talent as a singer, and feature the first recorded example of scat singing.

These records were the first to exploit Armstrong's talent as a singer. One famous example is "Heebie Jeebies," which contains what is probably the first recorded example of scat singing, that is, wordless vocalizing that improvises on a jazz theme. Louis always insisted that the reason he scatted his way through "Heebie Jeebies" is that he dropped the sheet music and couldn't remember the words.

Armstrong's gravelly voice—the "big fish horn voice" that Fletcher Henderson was afraid to unleash—was an immediate hit. It was also astonishingly influential to other singers. As Gary Giddins notes:

> It would be another four years before singers realized how versatile his voice was, but from the moment Louis' "novelty" vocal hit the street, other

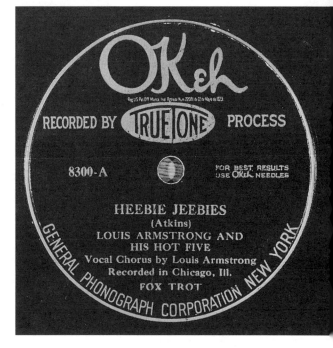

musicians were, in Earl Hines' recollection, sticking their heads out the window trying to catch colds to sound like Louis.[53]

Armstrong was soon singing on other people's records, even though he was under exclusive contract to OKeh. Unfortunately, his voice was so distinctive that it was impossible to disguise it. At one point, Armstrong made some records under Lil's name for a rival company. The OKeh executives called him in and asked who he thought the mystery singer might be. Louis replied, "I don't know, but I won't do it again."[54]

Leaving Chicago

A reform movement in government took hold of Chicago in 1927 and 1928. Many speakeasies were closed and there were hard times for musicians. Soon, the Great Depression would contribute to a slump in recordings as well. In 1929, Louis found himself out of work and broke.

New York was the obvious place to go. Several things helped. His recordings provided Armstrong with a wider audience than he had in Chicago. The publication of two books, *125 Jazz Breaks for Cornet* and *50 Hot Choruses for Cornet*—transcriptions of Louis's playing printed by the Melrose Music Company—helped spawn a generation of imitators.

Armstrong's book, 50 Hot Choruses for Cornet, *enabled musicians everywhere to imitate the famous musician. The book helped to bring Armstrong out of a slump after the Chicago music scene turned bleak.*

Finally, one more thing conspired to lure him back to New York: OKeh's new recording director, Tommy Rockwell. Rockwell was personable, charming, and a ruthless salesman. But he didn't know anything about music, and he had a notorious tin ear. Rockwell was based in New York, and in 1929, he sent Armstrong a telegram urging him to come back East.

5 Broadway and Beyond, 1929-1932

The next years of Armstrong's life were chaotic. He was one of the best-known black musicians alive, a hero to thousands of African Americans, and one of the few black performers who worked steadily during the Great Depression. He appeared in a hit Broadway revue, made a successful West Coast appearance, produced some fine recordings, and staged a triumphant return to his hometown.

But there were also problems. His managers overworked him to the point of exhaustion. He had continuing health problems. He was arrested for marijuana use. His marriage ended, and a subsequent relationship was tempestuous. And his sidemen were a constantly changing group with varying abilities, not a stable group of professionals.

Louis agreed to leave Chicago for New York on one condition. He wanted to bring his musician friends with him. He'd been through some tough times with "the boys" from the Carroll Dickerson band,

Armstrong (standing) and his band in 1929. Loyal to many of the band's members, Armstrong insisted on bringing them with him to New York.

and he was loyal. "I was one guy who always stuck with a bunch of fellows," he remarked later, "especially if I liked them."[55]

Lil scraped together twenty dollars each for the band's traveling money, although she was staying behind. They loaded their equipment into four ancient cars and took off by way of Detroit, Toledo, Cleveland, Buffalo, and Niagara Falls. Drummer Zutty Singleton remembers, "That was some trip. We had a couple of vibraphones—tied them on the car and they got all rusty. . . . We didn't know nothin'."[56]

One measure of their innocence about life on the road was their surprise at discovering their own fame. They were

---

His Own Man

Louis made some concessions to others in his life, but never in the way he played his music. As James Lincoln Collier notes in his biography of Armstrong:

"[I]t was almost impossible to tell him how he should play and behave on the stand. Throughout his career he allowed others to choose sidemen for him, to pick tunes for him, to make arrangements for him. But once he was on the bandstand, he was in charge. He set the tempos, called the tunes, played them as he wished, and did whatever clowning around he chose to do.

Dave Gold, from the [Joe] Glaser office, said, 'He was a stubborn guy. To me he was gracious, nice, pleasant, yet he could also be tough, tough on the people around him to make sure they did the job right.' Joe Sully, also from the Glaser office, who booked Armstrong for a period, said, 'You couldn't tell him what to do on the stage. . . . [It was] the one thing he fought for. He wanted to do his show.' He would even fight off suggestions from Joe Glaser, whom in other respects he allowed complete control of his career. Give him a song and he would sing it; but tell him *how* to sing it and he would chase you out of the room.

This is not to say that people around him did not push him in commercial directions. Glaser was always telling Armstrong to 'make faces.' Glaser said, 'I used to say, "Louis, forget all the goddamn critics, the musicians. Play for the public. Sing and play and smile. Smile, goddamnit, smile. Give it to them."' And, of course, his recording directors were interested in hits, not great jazz, by and large. Nonetheless, Armstrong alone decided what he was going to do on the stand."

Amstrong's band found work at some of the hottest nightspots in Harlem, which burst with thriving dance clubs.

used to being stars in Chicago. They hadn't realized, however, that records and radio broadcasts had made them familiar to music fans across the country.

They were shocked to stop in small towns and hear their records playing from music shops and radios. Too late, they realized they could have booked some gigs along the way. Still, Louis was pleased to be warmly greeted everywhere. "We didn't know nothin' about radio then, or how far it reached. So it was all fun. The cats [in the small towns] were so glad to meet us that we didn't need spending money."[57]

Along the way, cars crashed or died and were abandoned. By the time they reached New York City, they were down to one vehicle—Louis's Hupmobile. When it overheated in Times Square and the radiator cap blew off, a policeman came over to investigate and ended up searching the car for shotguns. He'd seen the Chicago license plates and assumed the worst.

The First Gigs

Tommy Rockwell was upset when Louis arrived with a whole band. He'd booked Louis as a solo act, and had no desire to be responsible for a crowd. But Louis was confident they'd find work, and insisted that Rockwell give them money to see them through.

Within two weeks, they did find work—first at a Bronx club replacing Duke Ellington's band, and then at a Harlem nightspot called Connie's Inn. Connie's was one of the hottest clubs in Harlem, at a time when it seemed like every block there had a thriving joint.

Like the Cotton Club, Connie's was famous for sophisticated shows that combined comedians, dancers, singers, and chorus girls.

Louis's brushes with crime didn't end when he left Chicago. The club's owners, Connie Immerman and his brother George, were not directly related to New York's gangland activity, but (like Tommy Rockwell) they had connections with a hood named Owney Madden.

Rockwell had arranged for Louis to appear in a revue called "Great Day." Armstrong took a leave from the Dickerson band to begin work on it in Philadelphia. The composer was a well-known songwriter, Vincent Youmans, and the band was Fletcher Henderson's top-notch group. But rehearsals did not go well, and when the show opened, it was a bomb. Louis returned to the Dickerson fold.

Early in his stay on the East Coast, Louis also took part in what was probably one of the very first mixed-race recording sessions. It was organized by a well-respected white guitarist named Eddie

Condon. The players included a white trombonist, Jack Teagarden, who would later become an important part of Armstrong's All-Stars band.

Armstrong also recorded with a nine-piece band led by another musician who would become important to him—the Panamanian-born Luis Russell. This session marked Louis's first foray into pop music, as opposed to straight jazz. The tune was "I Can't Give You Anything But Love (Baby)." It was a big hit, and from then on, Armstrong began paying attention to the pop market.

"Hot Chocolates"

Soon after "Great Day" flopped, two well-known musicians, lyricist Andy Razaf and composer-performer Fats Waller, opened a new revue at Connie's Inn. It was called "Hot Chocolates." Louis joined the revue's pit band, that is, the group that accompanies a stage show from the orchestra pit.

Eddie Condon (on guitar) organized Armstrong and other well-known musicians for one of the first mixed-race recording sessions.

Lyricist Andy Razaf (left) and composer-performer Fats Waller (right) opened the "Hot Chocolates" revue at Connie's Inn. Armstrong was a member of the pit band for the successful revue, which later played 219 performances on Broadway.

He was given a new song to sing between acts. It would become one of Razaf and Waller's most famous tunes: "Ain't Misbehavin'." At first, Louis merely sang the number while standing in the orchestra pit. But it was such a hit with audiences that the show's producers moved him onstage and put him in another number. The title of this trio with singer Edith Wilson and Fats Waller reflected the ample girth of its three singers: "Two Thousand Pounds of Rhythm."

The successful show moved to Broadway, where it played for 219 performances. It was also on at Connie's, however, so the performers had to race uptown every night after their Broadway appearance to make the late-night gig at Connie's.

"Hot Chocolates" didn't make Louis famous, but it did get him known to New York theatergoers. Also, Armstrong's hit recording of "Ain't Misbehavin'" helped bridge the gap between jazz and pop, preparing the way for the popular acceptance of jazz which was still to come.

The success of "Hot Chocolates" gave Rockwell some leverage in dealing with club owners. As Armstrong's reputation grew, however, Rockwell started to overbook him. The extra gigs and recording sessions, in addition to the already hectic Broadway-Connie's commute, began to exhaust the trumpeter.

Rockwell also began pressuring him to drop the Dickerson band. When "Hot Chocolates" closed, Armstrong joined Luis Russell's band as the frontman. He felt badly about the split, and longtime friends, like Zutty Singleton, never forgave him for it, but Armstrong bowed to Rockwell's decision.

An offer to play at a club in Los Angeles came just at the right moment, when Armstrong was feeling overworked and pressured in New York. In the summer of 1930, he began an extended engagement with the Les Hite band at the new Cotton Club in Culver City, a suburb of Los Angeles.

In most respects, this first trip of Armstrong's to the West Coast was successful. Culver City was an oasis of quiet after New York. He had a simple schedule, without travel or doubling between theaters. And he liked the climate.

He remained in California through the following spring. During his stay, Armstrong made his first appearance in a movie, performing and playing for an obscure film called *Ex-Flame*. He made some of his best big-band recordings. He also made his last record as a sideman: "Blue Yodel Number Six," by country singer Jimmie Rodgers. Many years later, when Louis made an album of country tunes, he'd joke that he'd been playing country for decades.

Armstrong meshed well with the Hite band, and their regular radio broadcasts helped spread his popularity. Lawrence Brown, a trombonist who played in that band, recalls:

> He was the kind of musician you could sit there all night and listen to and be amazed at the technique, the poise, and just everything. People used to come from way up around Seattle to hear him. Every trumpet player at that time tried to play one of his choruses.[58]

A Drug Bust

But not everything went well on the West Coast. In November 1930, Armstrong was arrested for drug possession.

Louis never used hard drugs and drank only lightly. But he was fond of marijuana—as were many jazz musicians of that

Armstrong (seated, right) with the Les Hite band at the Cotton Club in Culver City. Armstrong enjoyed the band's relaxed schedule. At the same time, the band's regular radio broadcasts fueled Armstrong's popularity.

Lawrence Brown, a trombonist who played in the Les Hite band, once remarked of Armstrong, "He was the kind of musician you could sit there all night and listen to and be amazed."

era—and he was a lifelong user. (In his later years, he even wrote President Eisenhower a letter urging that it be made legal.) He often remarked that he liked it because it was a natural herb, like those his mother gave him to remedy childhood illnesses.

The drug bust was probably a setup. It may have been arranged by a rival nightclub owner. Armstrong and a friend, a white drummer named Vic Berton, were arrested while smoking pot in Louis's car one night between shows. They spent the night in jail, and the next day each received six months' probation and a thousand-dollar fine. In addition, Armstrong had to publicly declare he'd never smoke pot again.

The two were treated well by the policemen who recognized and respected Armstrong. Louis later recalled that one cop admitted on the way downtown that he and his family listened to Armstrong's broadcast every night. He promised that Louis and his friend wouldn't be roughed up.

The light sentences they received may have been because Abe Lyman, who led the band Berton played with, intervened. But it may also have been because Tommy Rockwell sent a man named Johnny Collins to Los Angeles to straighten things out.

Like Rockwell, Collins was bluntmannered and foulmouthed. Collins convinced Armstrong that he and Rockwell had cut a deal, and that he, Collins, was now Louis's manager. In fact, Collins was simply trying to muscle his way into being Louis's manager.

The California trip was unfortunate in another way. It crystallized the problems between Louis and Lil. When she came to visit him, he discovered that she was having an affair in Chicago. Meanwhile, Alpha was pressuring Louis. He and Lil decided to finally separate, although they would not divorce for another seven years.

Gangster Trouble

Armstrong returned to Chicago in the spring of 1931, to a club Collins booked for him. Armstrong put together a ten-piece band—the first big band he'd formed on his own, instead of inheriting one ready-made.

He appointed another trumpeter, Zilner Randolph, as its music director. Armstrong often remarked later that this was the happiest band he ever led. "Now there's a band that really deserved a whole lot of credit that they didn't get. They made some of my finest recordings with me."[59]

When Rockwell heard Armstrong was under Collins's wing, he sent some men to bring the musician back to New York. As Armstrong told the story later, a man appeared in his dressing room one night and told him that they were going to New York. Louis said he had no intention of going to New York, whereupon the man pulled out a gun. Louis then said that he might have to reconsider.

Armstrong arranged for Johnny Collins to sneak him and his band out of Chicago later that night. The band made its way to Louisville, where it performed on the eve of the Kentucky Derby—the first black band to play the rooftop club of the Kentucky Hotel. Since Louis didn't feel safe playing in either Chicago or New York, the band then continued south, playing a string of one-nighters. Collins had arranged a homecoming for Louis in New Orleans.

Back to New Orleans

A huge celebration was held for Armstrong's first visit home in nine years. A large crowd and several marching bands met him at the station. Banners with slogans like "Welcome Home, Gates" lined the streets. A spontaneous parade escorted Louis and his band down Canal Street and around the city to their hotel.

While in town, Louis made a sentimental journey to the Waifs' Home and was reunited with family and friends from the Battlefield. He took time out to sponsor a baseball team, "Armstrong's Secret Nine." Louis recalled later that the team was never successful; they were so proud of their uniforms that they were afraid to get them dirty.

For the black community, Armstrong was a familiar and beloved figure. However, Collins had booked him into a whites-only club called the Suburban Gardens. The

During his stay in New Orleans, Armstrong sponsored a baseball team, "Armstrong's Secret Nine." The team competed in the Negro leagues, which gave blacks, barred at the time from the major leagues, an opportunity to play professional baseball.

When a white announcer refused to introduce Armstrong at the whites-only Suburban Gardens club in New Orleans, Armstrong decided to introduce himself. He was greeted with a standing ovation from the crowd.

people to whom Louis was a true hero—the black residents of New Orleans—couldn't see him play live. They could only line up on the levee outside the club—which they did, reportedly by the thousands—or listen to his nightly broadcasts.

One incident illustrates both Armstrong's irrepressible nature and the racism that was commonplace then. The white announcer who was scheduled to introduce Armstrong's first radio broadcast couldn't bring himself to do it. Backstage, he said, "I just haven't the heart to announce that nigger on the radio," and left.

Louis was no stranger to racism. He realized that for a white man to announce a black man in New Orleans in the 1930s was unusual. But the show had to go on, and Louis was determined not to be stopped.

For a black entertainer to announce himself was virtually unheard of, but Louis had no choice. He asked the band to play and hold one chord, then walked to the mike. He was met with such an ovation that several minutes passed before he could speak.

Then he introduced himself, thanked everyone for coming, and struck up a song that would become his signature tune: "When It's Sleepy Time Down South." Louis recalls:

> It was murder—one of my happiest days. For the rest of that night and the rest of that gig I did my own radio announcing. That other announcer? They threw him out the same night . . . ain't that something?[60]

Trouble on the Road

On his last night in New Orleans, Armstrong arranged to play a free show for his black fans on the grounds of a U.S. Army

Showman

Armstrong was always an all-around entertainer at heart, not a jazz purist. By the mid-thirties, as Gary Giddins points out, his singing and joking onstage was as important to his persona as his trumpet playing.

"Now he was . . . looking the audience in the eye when he sang, dramatizing the song, making it come alive as a vehicle for the fun and games of his incomparable extemporizations. His utterly original way of putting over a song—of selling it, of keeping the audience enchanted with it—was as instinctive and ingenious as any other aspect of his achievement. He figured out how to make his music part of a larger presentation, the Louis Armstrong Show. Like Bojangles [dancer-singer Bill Robinson], he offered a unique and prodigious talent; like him, too, he presented that talent as one aspect of a giant, all-encompassing personality that could absorb all the light in the room and shine it right back at the audience. 'The minute I walk on a bandstand, they know they're going to get something good. I see to that.'

Louis Armstrong never aspired to be a studied virtuoso who walks to center stage, bows, plays God's music, bows again, and leaves. He demanded a reaction whether he played for dancers or listeners. He thrived on the roar of the crowd, and like a great preacher or blues singer, he knew how to elicit the whoops and cries and moans of pleasure. . . . Armstrong was no longer [simply] one of the boys in the band. He was a musician, singer, bandleader, comic, dancer, actor."

base. Over a thousand people showed up, many of whom had traveled great distances in horse- or ox-drawn carts. Unfortunately, the crowd broke up before Louis could go onstage. Someone in the army ranks had decreed that no dancing was allowed on base, so the fans were cheated out of their concert and chased away.

Louis and his band ran into more trouble in Memphis, where they were thrown in jail. When they pulled into town in a decrepit bus, Johnny Collins's wife, Mary, happened to be sharing a front seat with guitarist Mike McKendrick. The sight of a white woman and a black man sitting in the same seat was too much for the authorities, and everyone spent a night in jail before Collins could bail them out.

The band continued its string of one-nighters, settled in St. Louis for a month, passed through Chicago again, and eventually decided to head back to New York in early 1932. Apparently, not all of Louis's business problems had been settled there; posters advertising all his engagements were immediately torn down. Armstrong was also hit with a lawsuit by Rockwell, who still claimed to be his manager.

In New York, Armstrong performed briefly in a new version of "Hot Chocolates" and began recording for the Victor Company. But mostly he was on the road for more one-nighters, and the uncertainty of that life was quickly felt. The band, which Armstrong had so enjoyed playing with, fell apart.

Overworked and Underpaid

One reason Armstrong's life was so hectic was because of the way that his managers treated him. Both Rockwell and Collins saw Armstrong as a meal ticket, not a gifted musician who deserved respect. As James Lincoln Collier notes:

> Today, entertainers of any economic promise are treated with the care given Venetian glass, but at that time handicaps were taken for granted, as part of the game.[61]

Besides constantly overbooking him, Armstrong's managers were willing to pay only for the cheapest musicians, not necessarily the best. There is also some evidence that they both cheated their client out of money. They also refused to let him rest so that his lip, which was constantly being overworked, could heal.

Louis had never learned how to minimize damage to his lip, a chronic problem for brass players. It would have required a year off for him to learn a proper embouchure (wind instrument technique) that would have prevented damage.

Armstrong—or his managers—couldn't afford a year off. The result was a constantly split and callused lip. Armstrong himself was partly responsible for this. He was a great believer in folk remedies. He would simply cut his calluses off with razor blades and then take a couple of months off. In between, he would apply lip salves that probably only helped a little.

He refused to listen to other musicians, who urged him to have a plastic surgeon remove the calluses. When he finally did consult a doctor late in his life, he had so many other health problems that the doctors could not safely operate. James Lincoln Collier notes, "Armstrong mistreated his lips to an incredible degree, probably more than any other professional trumpet player of his time."[62]

Louis did have a couple of operations in late 1936 and early 1937, in an attempt to correct another problem: nodes (growths) on his vocal cords. Unfortunately, the operations were not a success. The nodes were a problem that would plague him all of his life.

Louis's health problems during this period are evident in the recordings he made. On one tune, "Honey Do," the opening trumpet chorus was actually played by another musician because Louis's lip was in such bad shape. On other records, Louis had trouble making the high notes; he also sang off-key on occasion and generally sounded exhausted. Fortunately, this situation soon passed.

Armstrong was becoming popular and successful, but he was paying a price. It would not be for some time to come that his professional life would reach a pinnacle and that his personal life would stabilize.

6 Consolidating a Career, 1932-1943

The next period in Armstrong's life was a positive one. He toured Europe, made hit records, and began a fruitful relationship with a new manager. His popularity soared as he began appearing in films and concert halls. He also saw the pioneering music he had made in the mid-twenties achieve popularity as the swing era came in.

His personal life also improved. The marriage to Lil ended and another, to Alpha Smith, lasted only a short time. But a stable relationship soon began with Lucille Wilson, a dancer. Louis and Lucille would remain married for the rest of his life.

To Europe

In 1932, Armstrong embarked on a new phase of his career when Collins arranged for his first trip to Europe. Well-known musicians, like Sidney Bechet and Tommy Dorsey, had played there previously, but jazz was largely unknown in Europe. Armstrong's two early trips electrified Europeans, and the tour was a major milestone in jazz history.

This importance would have been hard to predict, though, given the haphazard nature of his first visit. The whole thing was arranged at the last moment, with only the vaguest of schedules. When Louis, Alpha, her mother, and Johnny and Mary Collins arrived in London, a hotel had not even been booked. A man from the music magazine *Melody Maker* had to quickly call around and find one.

Armstrong was booked into the Palladium theater. A group of expatriate American musicians came from Paris to be a "pickup" band—that is, one organized on the spot.

Critics and jazz fans loved Armstrong's first appearances. But he was not a success with all the Palladium patrons. Many walked out, puzzled by the strange sounds they heard. They weren't accustomed to such "rude" music, or to such intense energy from a performer.

After his run at the Palladium, a band of British musicians—the first white band Louis had played with—was hastily organized. This group toured briefly around England and Scotland. Louis then vacationed in Paris before sailing home in October 1932.

Armstrong had wowed the British fans, but at home he was still largely unknown outside the jazz community. In a letter to *Melody Maker* in early 1933, the influential American producer John Hammond wrote:

Armstrong was a big hit on his first European tour, wowing audiences who were unaccustomed to the electrifying sounds of jazz.

Louis as a person is just without equal in charm and general good nature. It's all the more unfortunate then that he is given insufficient publicity. It is a fact that when he came back from Europe there was not one line in any paper about it.[63]

Europe Again

Back in New York, besides gigs at Connie's Inn, Armstrong made a series of recordings with the brilliant drummer Chick Webb. This band would later achieve fame when Webb reorganized it around a young singer named Ella Fitzgerald. Unfortunately, the records Armstrong made with it were lukewarm, possibly because his lip was still bothering him.

In July 1933, Louis jumped at the chance to return to Europe. He opened at the Holborn Empire theater in London to great acclaim. In fact, Louis was so warmly received in London this time, that he briefly considered settling there.

One incident that soured him on the idea of settling in Europe, however, involved saxophonist Coleman Hawkins, who had played with Louis years before in the Henderson band and was now living in Paris. Hawkins was a star in his own right. It seemed like a good idea to pair these two giants in concert.

Armstrong, however, didn't think so. He balked at the prospect of sharing top billing but he didn't protest until after the concert had been set up. British jazz fans were upset by his refusal to perform, but, as James Lincoln Collier notes, they would have been less bewildered if they had seen him fending off competitors in the old days of the Sunset Cafe. "He was now unable to bear without strong emotion any threat to the loss of 'his' audience. Those people out there belonged to him, and he was not going to share them."[64]

Early on during this European jaunt, Armstrong broke his relationship with Collins. Armstrong had had enough of his manager's incompetence, rudeness, and alcohol problems. The final straw apparently was Louis's discovery that Collins had been shortchanging his musicians, had not paid Louis's U.S. taxes, and had not sent some promised money to Lil.

Jack Hylton, England's best-known bandleader, stepped into Collins's shoes.

A poster announces Armstrong's arrival at the Holborn Empire theater in London, where he opened his second European tour to great acclaim.

Hylton was a musician and more sympathetic to a musician's needs. He booked fewer performances for Louis and had him cut down on his high-note stage antics, so that by early 1934 his lip had healed considerably.

A high point during Armstrong's London engagement was when King George attended a performance. Louis dedicated his version of "I'll Be Glad When You're Dead, You Rascal You" to His Majesty. Louis looked up at the royal box, grinned, and said, "This one's for you, Rex."

The British press was scandalized that an American performer would have the nerve to speak to royalty that way. George, however, was charmed by Armstrong's remark. Louis recalls, "I was there in the cause of happiness, and he understood that. The King got to be one of the cats, or else he don't dig Satchmo."[65]

The Continent

Armstrong also toured Scandinavia, the Netherlands, France, Italy, and Switzerland. He even made a documentary in Denmark, which featured himself, with a Danish band, playing a piece based on traditional Eskimo songs from Greenland!

Louis was a big hit in Paris. He recalled later that "I had to take so many bows until I wound up taking 'em in my bathrobe."[66] He met the famous gypsy guitarist Django Reinhardt, leader of the house band at the Hot Club, and also recorded six tunes for a French label.

A French promoter arranged a heavy schedule for Armstrong through France, Italy, and Switzerland. Partway into the tour, Armstrong backed out—saying that

Armstrong and his band during a concert in Turin, Italy. Armstrong, scheduled next in Switzerland, cancelled the rest of the tour after his sore lip prevented him from performing.

his lip was too painful—and returned to Paris. N.J. Canetti, the promoter, was forced to cancel the Swiss part of the tour.

Canetti claimed that the real reason Louis backed out was that Armstrong resented the presence of two Americans in the show, pianist Herman Chittison and dancer Arita Day. But Arthur Briggs, an American trumpeter who lived in Paris, said that Armstrong's lip really was in bad shape. "His lips were as hard as a piece of wood and he was bleeding and everything else."[67]

Armstrong returned to New York in late 1934. He had to give up playing for six months because of his sore lip. Meanwhile, Canetti was suing him for breaking the European contract, and Lil was suing him for six thousand dollars in back maintenance. Tough times had returned.

When Armstrong resumed playing, he tried to front Chick Webb's band again. But Collins was still angry with Armstrong for breaking their relationship, and he sued Armstrong for breach of contract and forced him to leave New York. So it was back once more to Chicago.

The New Manager

The most important thing that came out of Armstrong's return to Chicago was that he hired Joe Glaser as his new manager. Joe, whom Louis had known since his days at the Sunset Cafe, continued to manage him for the rest of his (Glaser's) life. He also became in time the manager of many other important jazz musicians, including

Joe Glaser (left) remained Armstrong's trusted manager and close friend throughout his career.

work him, and there are no indications that he ever cheated his client.

As a manager, Glaser played hardball. He was not above bribery or threats. He would sometimes force record companies to accept other acts he managed in order to keep their top draws, such as Armstrong. He was notorious for signing potential Armstrong rivals to exclusive contracts, then putting a freeze on their careers to nullify their potential.

But he was also a private and reserved man and considered fair by many who dealt with him. He never had a contract with Armstrong. No one knows what percentage Glaser took of Armstrong's earnings, but they both became millionaires. Armstrong himself rarely even voiced an opposite opinion to Glaser's. It was enough that Glaser took the business pressure off him and allowed him to simply create.

Glaser worked hard for Armstrong right from the start. He began booking his client into the best theaters and negotiating lucrative recording deals. As a result of Glaser's efforts, Armstrong also began getting roles in feature films and became the first African American to have a national network radio show.

Duke Ellington, Dinah Washington, and Billie Holiday.

Like Armstrong's other managers, Glaser was a tough guy. Glaser was at least indirectly connected with organized crime in the old Sunset Cafe days, and it is possible that the connection continued. Unlike the others, however, Glaser played it straight with Armstrong. He didn't over-

Glaser worked hard for Armstrong, booking him into many of the best theaters. His efforts paid off—Louis began getting film roles and became the first African American to have a national network radio show.

Nor was Glaser content to sit at home while his prize client worked. He made a point of traveling regularly with Armstrong and his musicians on their bus. This was an unusual and sometimes dangerous thing for a white man to do in those days, given the treatment that was sometimes received by blacks.

The two men developed a kind of love between them. They did not socialize much, but they spoke regularly on the phone—and they trusted one another. As Armstrong puts it:

> Always remember this one thing. Anything that I have done musically since I signed up with Joe Glaser . . . it was his suggestion. Or order, whatever you may call it. With me, Joe's words were law.[68]

Armstrong also reconnected in Chicago with his former music director, Zilner Randolph. They assembled a band that toured the Midwest and South. The band broke up in New York and Armstrong rejoined Luis Russell's band for a winter-long engagement.

Things were beginning to look up. Armstrong had a steady band and a reliable musical director. He had regular work and a manager who treated him well. He also had a new contract with Decca Records that let him record frequently.

European Gamble

Armstrong took a big chance in leaving the United States for his first trip to the unknown territory of Europe. Max Jones and John Chilton write in their biography of Armstrong that the initial reaction in England was disappointing.

"Hopes and plans soon foundered and it would hardly have surprised the people close to him if he had retired hurt and returned home after the setbacks which followed his initial engagement. But he accepted the vicissitudes with good humor, shrugging off the disappointments and reveling in the successes. When he did return, four months later, he may not have been much richer than when he left; but he had a new concept of the importance of jazz, and increased confidence in his own musical status. For this and other reasons the visit was to prove a turning point in his career. Like most of his decisive moves it was made at the ideal moment, though this was not apparent for some time. . . .

Armstrong's playing was at a peak at the time. . . . His technique was in miraculous working order. . . . As a jazz player he had it all; all, that is, except widespread recognition as a creative musician. That was something he picked up in Europe, and not overnight."

Armstrong and Luis Russell during a recording session for Decca Records in 1935. Armstrong's reunion with Russell and his recording contract with Decca marked an upturn in Armstrong's career.

For once, he could tend to his physical health and concentrate just on playing.

Changing Styles

There had been rough times, but Armstrong was one of the few black performers who worked steadily during the Great Depression. In part, this was because of the organized-crime connections of his managers. But a more important reason was that he was willing and able to change his style.

As jazz and pop moved closer together, Armstrong became an unashamed pop performer—as much an entertainer and singer as a pure jazzman. By making this transition, he survived both professionally and artistically. "Had Louis not changed his repertoire," Max Jones and John Chilton write, "he would have sunk into obscurity like so many jazzmen."[69]

Armstrong had been singing pop songs since early in his career and had first recorded one in 1928: "St. James Infirmary." By the mid-thirties, he had recorded a great many hits that straddled the worlds of jazz and pop, including "I Can't Give You Anything But Love (Baby)," "Ain't Misbehavin'," "Black and Blue," and "When You're Smiling."

Armstrong had a gift for turning even the dullest tune into something moving and memorable. He often said that there was no such thing as a bad song. This, many feel, is one sure sign of his artistic genius. As Gary Giddins notes, his remark was "much as van Gogh might have said there are no bad colors."[70]

Meanwhile, the music called swing was taking the world by storm. Swing was characterized, of course, by a "swinging" tempo, which made it ideal for dancing, and by the interplay between the brass and reed sections of a band.

When Benny Goodman, Glenn Miller, and other bandleaders popularized swing in the mid-thirties, it was not new. Bandleaders like Fletcher Henderson, Duke Ellington, and Paul Whiteman had been refining the swing sound for years. The public simply caught up with them.

But Goodman's band led the way for mass acceptance, and by 1938, "the King of Swing" was selling out Carnegie Hall. Ironically, years before, Armstrong's Hot Five and other pioneering bands had done much to lay the musical groundwork for swing.

Louis finally divorced Lil in 1938. He then married Alpha, but they soon broke up. The relationship that had been so compatible when they were sweethearts didn't work as a marriage. They were divorced in 1942.

Lucille Wilson

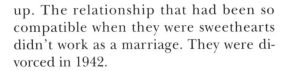

That year, Armstrong was working in a revue at the Cotton Club. A pretty dancer in the show, Lucille Wilson, caught his eye. Lucille, who had grown up in a middle-class neighborhood in Corona in the New York borough of Queens, danced to support her mother, two brothers, and a sister.

To supplement her income, Lucille also sold cookies to the members of the show. One night, Lucille came into Louis's

Pioneered by such performers as Armstrong and Paul Whiteman (pictured), the swing sound became extremely popular in the mid-thirties. Often played by big bands like this one, the music's "swinging" tempo made it ideal for dancing.

Wowing the Fans

Armstrong met with mixed success among the general populace on his first trip to England—but he knocked out the hard-core jazz fans, who had never seen anything like him. In The Louis Armstrong Story, *writer Max Jones describes witnessing Armstrong's show at London's Palladium theater.*

"What I can call to mind is an image of the man out front—a lithe, smallish but power-packed figure prowling the stage restlessly, menacingly almost, and growling and gesticulating when he was not playing, singing, or talking into the microphone. He addressed the trumpet as though it had a life of its own ('Speak to 'em, Satchelmouth'), and controlled the band with faintly alien instructions like 'Way down, way down,' 'Keep muggin'' . . . 'lightly, lightly and politely,' and 'swing, swing, swing, you cats.' Each tune was climaxed with outbursts of prodigious bravura [virtuoso] trumpet. . . . I remember doubting if he was in full control of himself. Reviewers everywhere pulled out the stops to describe Louis' act, and a great deal was made of him 'striding and sweating all over the stage' and mopping up with a succession of handkerchiefs."

dressing room to deliver his regular box of cookies. To impress her, Louis said that he'd buy as many cookies as she could make, every night. He'd then donate them, he said, to Harlem schoolchildren.

His ploy worked. Lucille and Louis began going out together regularly. They married in October 1942, not long after they'd met, and remained so for the rest of Louis's life.

Lucille understood that music was Louis's first love. She didn't dominate his business decisions, as Lil had done—Joe Glaser was there for that. And she was a compatible personality. As Armstrong writes in an unpublished memoir, "It seemed to me that Lucille was the ideal girl for me. In fact our lives were practically the same."[71]

Lucille took care of every need—even to the point of remembering names for Louis. His habit was to call everyone "Pops," even close friends. That way, he didn't need to remember the hundreds of people he met while touring. As Louis remarked in an interview, "She knows all the bigwigs by name. All I have to do is say 'Who's this cat?' and before I look around she's answered, 'Oh, Vouty-Vouty,' sump'n like that. Beautiful memory, Lucille."[72]

Lucille was even willing to overlook Louis's occasional extramarital affairs. She once said in an interview:

Let's say the eye sees what it wants to see. There are all sorts of women in the entertainment field. They throw their arms around Louis. I have partial vision on purpose.[73]

The House

In the spring of 1943, Lucille talked Louis into buying a house. The neighborhood was Corona, the largely black community in Queens where Lucille had grown up.

Armstrong didn't like the idea at first. He spent 90 percent of his time on the road, and he didn't see much point to owning a place. Still, he gave her permission to buy a house while he was away on tour.

He was still skeptical when he arrived back at New York's Penn Station. First he took a cab to Harlem, where he hung out with friends before calling his new home. He asked Lucille to wait outside; if he didn't like what he saw, he'd leave. When the cab pulled up in front, Louis tipped the driver but asked him to wait.

Lucille wasn't outside. He rang the bell and she opened the door, saying, "Welcome home, honey." She escorted Armstrong from room to room. She'd redecorated each and prepared an elaborate meal, as well.

Armstrong was speechless. He ran to the cab and invited the driver in for dinner. The three of them ate and drank for the next three or four hours.

Louis loved the house, though he never spent much time there. His study became a refuge for writing and listening. He had never owned any records—even his own—but once he was settled he began a collection. He also began taping performances, conversations, radio broadcasts, and home concerts. Louis's handmade catalog of tapes and records eventually ran to 175 pages.

In later years, the quality of the neighborhood declined. Armstrong was rich, and could have lived anywhere. Lucille and Glaser tried to get him to move to Long Island, but he refused. He said he

Louis and Lucille at their wedding reception in 1942. Louis gave much of the credit for the success of their marriage to Lucille, who he described as "the ideal girl for me."

liked being close to Shea Stadium where the Mets played—although he also made public his disappointment that he'd never been invited to sing the National Anthem for his favorite team.

He loved to sit on the stoop or watch TV with the neighborhood kids. Louis never had children of his own, but he enjoyed the company of children. He wrote in 1970:

> We've both seen three generations grow up on our block. White & black, and those kids, when they grew up and got married, their children still come around to our house and visit their friends Louis and Lucille.[74]

Recordings and Movies

This was a prolific recording period for Armstrong. His new label, Decca, was very commercially oriented. As a result, Armstrong recorded everything from spirituals to country, Christmas novelties, and even Hawaiian songs. He was also teamed frequently with other artists, including Ella Fitzgerald, the Mills Brothers, Billie Holiday, and Bing Crosby.

The best of the Decca records were made with the Luis Russell Orchestra. It included such fine musicians as drummer Big Sid Catlett, bassist Pops Foster, and trombonist J.C. Higginbotham. Armstrong later remarked:

> There were several boys from my hometown [in that band], so you can imagine how well I felt at home with them. . . . I was very proud and happy to have played in the band every night.[75]

Armstrong in front of his Corona home in 1960, where he lived until his death. Over the years, the quality of the neighborhood declined. Yet Armstrong refused to give up his beloved home, where he often watched the goings-on from his steps and enjoyed the company of neighborhood kids.

Bing Crosby was the star of Armstrong's first significant movie. Louis had previously been in a few musical shorts, as

The White Handkerchief

By the early thirties, Armstrong's trademark white handkerchief—he used as many as six per tune—was already a standard stage prop. In The Louis Armstrong Story, *Max Jones writes:*

"The white linen squares served a purpose besides the principal one—a useful bit of stage business which worked in the spotlight and helped to keep the customers' eyes on Louis. (Maybe the handkerchief had taken on a symbolic meaning for him, as the white gardenia did for [singer] Billie Holiday.) Then again . . . a musician who worked in one of his [later] bands claimed that the handkerchief in Louis' left hand could fulfill another function: used in a certain fashion toward the end of a number, it indicated which of two possible endings the trumpeter would choose."

Armstrong appeared with Bing Crosby in a number of commercially successful movies, including Pennies from Heaven *and* Doctor Rhythm *(pictured).*

well as the ill-fated *Ex-Flame* and the Danish documentary. But an appearance in *Pennies from Heaven* in 1936 was his big break.

It was followed by *Everyday's a Holiday* with Mae West, *Doctor Rhythm* with Crosby, and *Artists and Models* with Jack Benny. Most of these movies were commercially successful. Racism, however, still reared its ugly head in Armstrong's career—his appearances were often cut from the final version of a film when it played in the Deep South or overseas.

In 1938, Armstrong recorded a then little-known spiritual from his youth, "When the Saints Go Marching In." His sister, Mama Lucy, criticized him for jazzing up a church piece. Louis replied that she played bingo in church, and what was the difference? "Saints" would, of course, become one of Louis's most famous songs and the best known of all tunes associated with New Orleans.

7 The All-Star Years, 1943-1957

Armstrong saw the war years through with a series of appearances on military bases. Afterwards, his appearance in a movie, *New Orleans*, helped spark a revival in Dixieland music. Out of this grew the All-Stars, his small, New Orleans-style band. It represented a major shift away from the large orchestras he'd previously played with for most of his career.

The All-Stars changed personnel many times, not always to the best musical advantage. But the early groups, which included some fine musicians, recorded some brilliant work. Armstrong continued to perform with this band until his death.

The Rise of Bebop

The United States entered World War II late in 1941. A recording ban was imposed in 1942. Instead of making records, Armstrong put his energy into appearing on military bases in benefit performances. He made extensive broadcasts on the AFRS (Armed Forces Radio Service) network, and also produced a number of "V-discs," special recordings for use by the military.

The forties were a turbulent time for jazz. The main change was that swing was superseded by a new phenomenon called bebop. Bebop combined sophisticated harmonic and rhythmic ideas with fast, furious, often wild improvisation.

The new music was closely associated with the beatniks, and the bebopper's classic outfit—beret, goatee, blue jeans—became a model for all self-respecting hipsters. Its primary performers included trumpeters Dizzy Gillespie and Miles Davis, pianists Bud Powell and Thelonious Monk, saxophonist Charlie Parker, and drummer Max Roach.

These musicians were demanding respect as serious artists. Many of them saw Armstrong as an old fuddy-duddy, a relic of the vaudeville era. As Gary Giddins puts it, "He had too much fun out there [onstage]. It was embarrassing. Artists don't grin and mug and roll their eyes."[76]

Bebop was difficult to grasp and not appealing to everybody. To most older musicians, including Armstrong, it seemed out of control. He referred to it as "Chinese music" and "monkey-shine business." He could not understand the appeal of music that seemed, to him, deliberately cold and distant.

But it was gaining in popularity, and as a result, his own bookings were down. He had a solid audience, but his popularity was not skyrocketing as in the thirties. Also, he was finding it increasingly difficult to tour with a large orchestra.

The forties ushered in a new fast-paced, wildly improvised style of jazz called bebop, popularized by such performers as saxophonist Charlie Parker (center) and trumpeter Miles Davis (right).

Younger jazz fans no longer attended Armstrong's shows or bought his records. He had become old-fashioned. He needed something different.

New Orleans at the Movies

In 1946, Louis took part in a film, *New Orleans*, which purported to be about the birth of jazz. It was not much of a movie—just a silly love story with music, starring Bing Crosby.

Barney Bigard, a New Orleans native, was one of the musicians who appeared in the movie. In his memoirs, he writes that Louis was the only actor on the set who was allowed to improvise dialogue.

> Louis, well they just let him be Louis. They let him have his head as to the personality he played in the film. . . . He could say anything and get away with it, and the movie people would just laugh and enjoy it.[77]

Seen from today's perspective, *New Orleans* seems insulting. For one thing, it implies that the birth of jazz was a matter of simple black people handing over a native music to white aristocracy. It also gives little attention to the dignity of its black performers; the exquisite singer Billie Holiday, for instance, is cast as a maid.

But *New Orleans* did serve one useful purpose: it put Louis firmly in the national spotlight when it opened in 1947. A lot of attention was focused on him and on classic New Orleans-style Dixieland music—a style that, in fact, he had not played for many years.

Birth of the All-Stars

Initially, it was Joe Glaser's idea to form a small Dixieland combo. He noticed how well the small-band format had worked on the movie set, and he thought the time was ripe for a revival of Dixieland.

Armstrong, Barney Bigard (far right), and other well-known musicians all came together to appear in New Orleans. *While the movie was in some ways insulting in its implications about the birth of jazz, it put Armstrong back in the national spotlight.*

Armstrong himself was tired of fronting a big band. He welcomed the idea and gave all the credit to Glaser.

> It was Joe's idea. After all, he's the man who has guided me all through my career. Coming from the man I love, who I knew was in my corner, it was no problem for me to change.[78]

A prominent writer and composer, Leonard Feather, organized a Carnegie Hall concert in early 1947 that crystallized the change. In the first half of the concert, Armstrong was accompanied by a small band led by New Orleans clarinetist Edmond Hall. In the second half, he played with a big band. Soon after, promoter Ernie Anderson organized another concert at Town Hall that was, essentially, the first performance of Louis Armstrong and His All-Stars.

The Town Hall concert was a smash success—the biggest standing-room-only sellout the hall had seen in years. The band included such fine musicians as Jack Teagarden, the laconic trombonist whom Louis had known for years, and drummer Big Sid Catlett.

Louis played nearly thirty tunes during the course of the evening, spanning his entire career from early jazz to the latest film tunes, and brought the house down. As Gary Giddins notes, "It was the kind of triumph that can determine the direction of an artist's career."[79]

In the fall of 1947, Glaser arranged an engagement at a Los Angeles club called Billy Berg's. Vocalist-comedian Velma

One of the All-Stars' many "all-star" lineups: (left to right) Cozy Cole, Jack Teagarden, Armstrong, Arvell Shaw, Barney Bigard, and Earl Hines.

Middleton was added to the band. These performances were sold out every night. The attendant publicity, coming hard on the heels of the Town Hall and Carnegie Hall shows, shot Armstrong straight back into the spotlight. From then on, he could name his price.

In early 1948, he played another historic show, this time at a festival in Nice, France. Besides the leader, Teagarden, Middleton, and Catlett, the band included clarinetist Barney Bigard, bassist Arvell Shaw, and an old acquaintance of Louis's who was both a friend and a rival—pianist Earl "Fatha" Hines. This would become the first official lineup of the All-Stars—and also, many fans argue, the best.

The All-Stars

For years, despite shifting personnel, the All-Stars really was a band of all stars. On trombone, Louis had, in succession, Jack Teagarden, who was also a sly and funny vocalist, Trummy Young, and Tyree Glenn; on clarinet, Barney Bigard and Edmond Hall; on piano, Earl Hines and the stylish Billy Kyle; on drums, Sid Catlett and Cozy Cole; on bass, Milt Hinton, a majestic player, and the young and energetic Arvell Shaw.

The All-Stars were, in their time, the highest paid jazz combo in the world. The lineup of musicians was a traditional New

A Showman's Glamorous Life

As Armstrong points out in this passage from Louis Armstrong—A Self-Portrait, *being a famous and globe-trotting musician has its downside.*

"[I]f somebody back in New Orleans had said, 'Now it's all going to be like that and such and that'—It would have scared me to death. Playing was fun then—and relaxed. Hit a bad note, so what? Nobody cared. Now, man, people in Europe can tell you everything you ever played, know every phrase, know everybody you ever made a record with. Can't let 'em down.

These days you got to look at it like a business. This life I got is very rough and few can do it. Now I'll come off five months on the road, have maybe a week off, then right back out. We don't have no days off—feel like I spent nine thousand hours on the bus, get off a bus, hop a plane, get in town just in time to play a gig, chops are cold, come off that stage too tired to raise an eyelash. Sometimes up at 5:30 the next morning to get to that next gig—just a whole lot of ringing and twisting and jumping and bumping and things."

The clowning and singing of vocalist-comedian Velma Middleton (center) were popular features of the All-Stars' performances.

Orleans instrumentation. But the music the band played was beyond category—with a diverse style and repertoire.

Louis's own tastes were broad. He liked to listen to everything, from opera to country. He never thought of himself as strictly a jazz musician, and he didn't like feeling hemmed in by such restrictions. He loved to shock jazz purists by proclaiming his love for such un-hip music as the ultra-sweet orchestra of Guy Lombardo.

A typical All-Stars concert usually opened and closed with two of Louis's signature tunes, "Indiana" and "When It's Sleepy Time Down South." In between, however, Louis would change the set list at a moment's notice, often without warning to his sidemen. As Lucille once remarked, he was closely tuned into an audience's feelings, and would change his set according to their wishes. "His mind worked so fast. He could hear gnats walking on cotton."[80]

The format was designed to provide a maximum of entertainment for the largest number of people. A show might include classic New Orleans numbers, such as "Tiger Rag" or "When the Saints Go Marching In." There would be solo spots

for the sidemen. Velma Middleton would sing and clown. Louis would sing a duet with "Tea"—perhaps "Lazybones," one of their best-loved collaborations. And Armstrong would always include a couple of then-current pop tunes.

The Personal Side

The All-Stars were professional to a fault, because Louis always insisted on it. He remembered the old days of New Orleans, when musicians would get so drunk onstage that they would forget where they were.

He also remembered the Fletcher Henderson orchestra and how disgusted he would get at the sloppiness of some of its members. Sometimes, musicians would get so far gone that they wouldn't show up for a gig on time, or at all.

Armstrong therefore established a lifelong habit of never drinking before a gig. This became an unspoken rule for the All-Stars. Barney Bigard recalled that Earl Hines loved cigars, but never smoked them onstage.

Of course in the All Stars there was never any smoking, or drinking for that matter, on the bandstand. We didn't need Joe Glaser to tell us that. I mean it just looked bad and we all made that rule ourselves.[81]

Armstrong himself was never late, and never seemed tired, stagestruck, or nervous on stage. Bigard remembers:

He would just come out laughing and waving his handkerchief. Sometimes, though [he might have been ill or tired], but you would never know it. He'd come out all smiles, and you thought he was having the biggest ball of his life.[82]

Armstrong's relationships with band members offstage ranged from friendly to merely cordial. As usual, he left the hiring and firing to someone else—in this case, Glaser—so that he could keep on an even keel with his musicians. As Bigard puts it, "He didn't want to tread on anyone's toes or hurt anyone's feelings, so he just made no comments on anything that happened."[83]

He had a solid friendship with Teagarden, even after Tea left the band to form his own group. Louis later recalled that when Tea joined the band

it was like a holiday—we understood each other so wonderful. There ain't going to be another Jack Teagarden. . . . He was from Texas, but it was always, "You a spade [black man], and I'm an ofay [white man]. We got the same soul. Let's blow"—and that's the way it was. He kept all his bad moments, his grievances, to himself. But I could tell his whole heart, his life, coming out of that horn. And it was all good.[84]

Things were not as smooth with another member of the early All-Stars, Earl Hines. Hines was used to being a bandleader

Armstrong and Jack Teagarden (pictured) shared a friendship based on mutual admiration and understanding.

himself, and he carried some lingering resentment from the old days in Chicago, when he and Armstrong had scuffled for work. Barney Bigard recalls:

> With our band you could feel the animosity between them. . . . [A]fter they would argue Earl would try to make things right with Louis. On the surface maybe he did, but Louis was like an elephant, he never forgot. . . . It was strange to me, because they made such great music together, and had respect for one another's music.[85]

Road Personality

On or off the road, Louis always had time for his fans, no matter how exhausted he

---

In the Dressing Room

Louis was at ease with a wide variety of people. In his biography of Armstrong, James Lincoln Collier quotes a friend of Armstrong's, New Orleans guitarist Danny Barker, describing a typical backstage scene:

"He be sittin' down in his underwear with a towel around his lap, one around his shoulders and that white handkerchief on his head . . . an' laughin' you know natural the way he is. And in the room ya see, maybe two nuns. You see a street walker dressed all up in flaming clothes. You see maybe a guy come out of a penitentiary. You see maybe a blind man sitting there. You see a rabbi, you see a priest, see. Liable to see maybe two policemen or detectives, see. You see a judge. All of 'em different levels of society in the dressin' room and he's talking to all of 'em.

'Sister so and so, do you know Slick Sam over there? This is Slick Sam, an ole friend of mine.' Now the nun's going to meet Slick Sam. Ole Notorious, been in nine penitentiaries. 'Slick Sam, meet Rabbi Goldstein over there, he's a friend of mine, rabbi good man, religious man. Sister Margaret do you know Rabbi Goldstein? Amelia, this is Rosie, good time Rosie, girl used to work in a show with me years ago. Good girl, she's a great performer. Never got the breaks.' Always a word of encouragement, see. And there'd be some kids there, white and colored. All the diverse people of different social levels . . . an' everybody lookin'. Got their eyes dead on him, jus' like they were lookin' at a diamond."

Armstrong and his wife Lucille receive a joyous welcome in Düsseldorf, Germany. Armstrong always made time for his friends and fans, and was well loved for his generosity and sense of humor.

might be. He always stopped to sign autographs, even when others in the band were yelling at him to hurry up before he missed his plane to the next gig.

Armstrong always carried two rolls of cash—one for himself, and one to hand out to those who came to him with a sob story. As Barney Bigard puts it:

> He was always good for a "touch." These musicians, old friends from New Orleans, even bums, would come to him and say, "Oh Louis, I don't have nothing to eat with in the morning" and he would peel them off some dollars.[86]

He had a huge sense of humor, and much of what he found funny was the kind of earthy humor he grew up with in New Orleans. One Christmas, Louis sent out thousands of cards that featured a smiling Satchmo sitting on the toilet. The text of the card was a kind of home-made advertisement for Louis's favorite laxative, an herbal concoction called Swiss Kriss.

Once, Louis's photographer friend, Jack Bradley, shot a nude photo of Louis from the back. Louis wanted thousands of copies printed up and sent to everybody he knew, but cooler heads (probably Lucille's) prevailed. On another occasion,

Bradley snuck up on him disguised in a full-face horror mask. Louis simply looked at him and mildly said, "Oh, Hi, Jack." When Bradley took the mask off, Louis looked again and screamed in terror.

Louis's genial good nature was evident most of the time. Only rarely would he lose his temper, and when he did, it was fierce. Guitarist Danny Barker once said, "Louis could get so mad he'd suck all the air out of a room." Lucille added, "I think he invented cuss words, he had some I've never heard before. But his anger was always justified—he didn't hold things in."[87]

Perhaps what made Louis the maddest was a threat to his musicianship. In 1953, Louis toured with Benny Goodman, in a highly publicized tour with great advance sales. Goodman let Louis know that it was his, Goodman's, gig, and that Louis would do as he was told. Louis's reply was to wait until the evening performance, where he outplayed Goodman so badly that Goodman literally got sick afterwards. Trumpeter Bobby Hackett, who was also on the tour, recalls, "Pops came close to killing him without touching him, just playing."[88]

The gigs, the money, and the honors had begun rolling in for Armstrong and

---

That Voice

Armstrong was without peer as a trumpet player and improvisor. But it was as a singer that he won the heart of the world. James Lincoln Collier notes that, even in the later part of his life, when his voice had deteriorated, his voice was what mattered.

"In April 1958, two nose and throat specialists from the University of Virginia heard Armstrong at a concert and, intrigued by the quality of his voice, asked permission to examine him. Armstrong was willing, and their report, which they sent to Louis' doctor, indicated that Armstrong was suffering from substantial leukoplakia with some polyploid changes—the 'growths' on the vocal cords, which had afflicted him for decades, perhaps since childhood.

However, the public seemed to find the rough voice [caused by the growths] attractive—it was lovable, endearing, as if a favorite teddy bear had got up on the bureau and started singing. But as we always discover in attempting to analyze Armstrong's musical qualities, there was something beyond the analyzable—an openness, a directness, that allowed listeners to look through the flesh to the light inside. You could warm your hands in front of Louis Armstrong. You could not be unhappy when he was singing."

Armstrong and Duke Ellington perform on Ed Sullivan's show. A superstar by the fifties, Armstrong became a regular guest on television variety shows.

the All-Stars from their first engagement, and they never really stopped.

A Superstar

By the end of the forties, Louis was a superstar. Throughout the fifties, he appeared in a feature movie about once a year. He was a guest on television variety shows six or eight times a year, including programs hosted by Ed Sullivan, Frank Sinatra, Milton Berle, and Nat "King" Cole. He broadcasted regularly on the radio from top nightclubs and drew capacity crowds for all his shows.

He recorded exclusively for Decca until 1954, when Glaser made him a freelancer. Glaser's emphasis was to find hits that would guarantee Armstrong radio play. On records, some of his best efforts were with singer Ella Fitzgerald.

In July 1950, *downbeat* magazine, the most important jazz magazine, devoted a special issue to Louis for his fiftieth birthday. In 1952, *downbeat*'s readers voted him "the most important musical figure of all time." In 1954, Japanese promoters awarded him the largest monetary guarantees for a performance ever given to an entertainer. The same year, he published a memoir about his early days in New Orleans, *Satchmo*, to generally good reviews.

He was so well known that even fan mail with only the skimpiest of addresses would reach him. Letters marked simply, "TO THE KING OF JAZZ, LOUIS ARMSTRONG, USA" or "TO OL' SATCHMO HIMSELF, WHEREVER HE IS" would routinely show up at his house in Queens.

8 Icon and Effigy in Music and Politics, 1957-1960

As Armstrong's fame as a musician increased, so did his role as a public figure. He was famous and highly visible and therefore an easy target for criticism. He caused a stir when he appeared in "blackface" during a Mardi Gras parade and an international incident when he spoke out about civil rights.

These controversies crystallized long-simmering resentments about his alleged "Uncle Tomming." An "Uncle Tom" is an African American who is seen as bowing to the wishes of white "masters." The name comes from Harriet Beecher Stowe's classic novel, *Uncle Tom's Cabin*. Armstrong's comical stage presence was often seen as promoting a "Tommish" image that many civil rights champions found distasteful.

Armstrong himself was usually indifferent to politics, and he usually brushed off racial controversy. He once remarked:

> Those people who make the restrictions, they don't know nothing about the music. It's no crime for cats of any color to get together and blow. Race-conscious jazz musicians? Nobody could be who really knew and loved the music.[89]

In 1949, the year that Armstrong made the cover of *Time* magazine, he caused an uproar by appearing as the King of the Zulus during Mardi Gras. He was invited to play the part of the king by the Zulu Aid Leisure and Social Club, one of the most prestigious of the New Orleans organizations that sponsored floats in the Mardi Gras parades.

Traditionally, the King of the Zulus wore huge white patches around his eyes and lips, a long wig, a crown, a red velvet gown with sequins, and a grass skirt. His job was to sit atop the float during the

Armstrong caused a public uproar when he appeared as the King of the Zulus on a Mardi Gras float.

Arkansas governor Orval Faubus called in the National Guard in an attempt to stop the desegregation of schools, defying a Supreme Court ruling.

parade, drinking champagne, and throwing coconuts to the crowd.

To Armstrong, being asked was like getting an honorary degree from a beloved school. As he put it, "It had been my lifelong dream to be the King of the Zulus, as it was the dream of every kid in my neighborhood."[90]

Many people, however, found the performance barbaric because of its racist "blackface" overtones; they saw it as demeaning to African-American dignity. Some newspaper writers, performers, and other public figures were openly critical of him. They saw the Zulu incident as part of Armstrong's ongoing problems with what they perceived as his "Uncle Tom" persona.

Still, the Zulu incident was a relatively small tempest, and it passed quickly. A later affair would have far more powerful repercussions.

Little Rock

Ironically, the thing that got Armstrong the most publicity in his life had nothing to do with music. Instead, it came when he spoke out against civil rights violations in the Deep South.

In 1954, a turning point in the American civil rights movement was reached. The Supreme Court ruled that "separate but equal" schools for black and white students were unconstitutional. Most public school boards complied with federal orders to desegregate.

The city of Little Rock, Arkansas, did not. In the fall of 1957, Arkansas governor Orval Faubus defied the Supreme Court ruling and swore that his schools would remain segregated. On September 17, an angry crowd gathered around nine black students who were attempting to attend classes at Little Rock's Central High School.

Faubus called in the National Guard to "maintain order" by barring the students from entering the school. The entire nation watched, spellbound, as TV crews recorded the tense situation. One person who was watching intently was Louis Armstrong. As it happened, he was in a hotel room in Grand Forks, North Dakota, where he was scheduled to perform that evening.

A Scoop in Grand Forks

The Grand Forks newspaper had assigned the task of interviewing Armstrong to one of its cub reporters—a student who was still in high school himself. He found the musician glued to the television set in his hotel room. When Armstrong saw a man spit in the face of a female student who was trying to walk to school, he could stand it no longer.

What followed was a long monologue, which the young reporter copied down as quickly as possible. Armstrong blasted President Eisenhower, calling him "two-faced" and "no-guts," because he had not taken decisive action. He called Faubus "an uneducated plowboy" and said that the governor's use of National Guard troops was a stunt "led by the greatest of all publicity hounds."[91]

The reporter knew he'd gotten a scoop—a famous entertainer, known for his genial nature, speaking out angrily on the most important current affair in the country. After he'd written the story, the newspaper's editor accompanied him to

Crowd members yell racial epithets at a student trying to pass through the lines of National Guardsmen in an effort to gain entrance to Little Rock's Central High School. Armstrong openly condemned President Eisenhower and Governor Faubus after seeing scenes like this on TV.

Armstrong's hotel to confirm the story's accuracy.

Armstrong read the entire story and approved it. He signed the copy paper to prove he had seen it. He also wrote the word "wild" and said to the editor, "That's just fine. Don't take nothin' out of that story. That's just what I said and still say."[92]

The Uproar

The story was picked up by the national wire services, and it created a sensation. Overnight, the most mild mannered of men was labelled as a fiery protester by observers around the world.

The next day, while Armstrong was asleep, his road manager, Pierre Tallerie, told reporters that Armstrong "was sorry he spouted off." When Armstrong found out, he fired Tallerie and made his own statement to the press:

> He's speaking for himself. My people—the Negroes—are not looking for anything—we just want a square shake. But when I see on television and read about a crowd in Arkansas spitting on a little colored girl—I think I have a right to get sore . . . do you dig me when I still say I have a right to blow my top over injustice?[93]

On September 23, Eisenhower finally took control by ordering the entire Arkansas National Guard into federal service. He then sent a thousand troops to Little Rock to enforce desegregation. It is probably too much to say that Armstrong's comments forced Eisenhower's hand—there was pressure on him from all sides—but they played at least a part in the president's actions.

Kidding the Interviewers

Armstrong never allowed himself to be pushed into saying something in public through leading questions. Even after the controversy over Little Rock broke, when many expected him to speak out seriously all the time, he kept things light and polite. In Satchmo, *Gary Giddins writes:*

"Armstrong shrugged off the idea that jazz was the private domain of blacks. . . . Urged by the commentator on a 1960 TV show to confirm the common observation that European jazzmen copied Americans, he snapped, 'We don't look at it that way. . . . How do we know who copied what?' He understood, as many didn't, that the strength of jazz lay in its international appeal and that chauvinistic hauteur [aloofness] implied constraints that were bad for business and for his musical message. By 1960 he was quick to insist that he was an 'ambassador' of music only and had nothing to do with politics. Yet his insistence on the universality of jazz was indisputably political. . . .

Sometimes he responded to interviewers who tried to feed him their own prejudices with the patience of a schoolmarm; sometimes he acquiesced and switched to a lighter subject. At his best he parried them with wit, as in a 1960 radio interview with British journalists in Kenya.

He was questioned about his vice. 'I do all the things that you do.'. . . About rock and roll. 'Oh, that's our church music.' About modern jazz. 'They make a thousand notes to get around the one.' About his appeal to the young. 'Yes, I'm young myself.' About his hectic schedule. 'I never felt yet that I didn't want to get on that stand.' About his popularity in Africa. 'Always have been Africans all over New Orleans.' About an East African song in his repertory. 'We like everything we play.' About how high he could go. 'Well, I can get up to p.'"

Armstrong was pleased by Eisenhower's move. He sent a wire to the White House that read, "If you decide to walk into the schools with the little colored kids, take me along, Daddy. God bless you."[94]

The State Department had been considering sending Armstrong on a tour of the Soviet Union. They hoped that a tour by black jazz musicians would help foster an image overseas of racially free America.

But Armstrong had said in Grand Forks that he'd cancel the tour, because "the way they are treating my people in the South, the government can go to

Eisenhower ordered the entire Arkansas National Guard into Little Rock to enforce desegregation. Armstrong's comments, which were condemned by many, may have played a part in the president's actions.

hell. . . . The people over there ask me what's wrong with my country, what am I supposed to say?"[95]

The State Department asked him to reconsider, but Armstrong refused. Benny Goodman, a white musician with a mixed band, eventually got the gig.

The attacks and defenses of Armstrong lasted for over a year. Several planned tours were scrubbed because of boycotts against Armstrong. A scheduled performance at the University of Arkansas was canceled by a student body vote. Armstrong was scheduled to perform with classical pianist Van Cliburn on television, but Cliburn's manager refused to let them play together.

But Armstrong also had many defenders during this period. Singer Eartha Kitt was among the first to publicly say that Louis was right to speak out. Trumpeter Max Kaminsky, then playing with Jack Teagarden's band, said:

> I think it was what Louis said that got Ike [Eisenhower] up off his rear over this Little Rock business. That episode is one hell of a smear over America, and it takes a hell of a lot of guts for Armstrong to stand up and say the things he said.[96]

Other entertainers were less kind, stating that Armstrong didn't understand anything about civic events. Louis's reply was, "Tell [them] I understand lynching, and that's a public event."[97]

Singer Eartha Kitt was one of the first entertainers to publicly defend Armstrong for speaking out against civil rights violations.

The Aftermath

Despite the criticism and the damage to his career, Armstrong continued to speak out. He was hurt and confused by the attacks against him, especially when they came from other African Americans.

He felt that he had long been a quiet pioneer for civil rights. As he points out in a 1967 interview in *Harper*'s magazine:

> As time went on and I made a reputation I had it put in my contracts that I wouldn't *play* no place I couldn't *stay*. I was the first Negro in the business to crack them big white hotels—Oh yeah! I pioneered, Pops![98]

Armstrong never actively took part in the civil rights marches of the sixties, however. About this decision, Lucille remarks:

> He gave money [to the civil rights cause], but there was no point in marching and getting his mouth bashed in. He was an artist first. He talked politics with me, and he was aware that every word he said had impact.[99]

One lingering effect of the controversy was that a secret FBI file on Armstrong remained active. The FBI had been keeping tabs on him since the late 1940s, because his name had turned up in the address book of someone they thought was suspicious, and because his name appeared on the letterhead of the Negro Actors Guild of America. They continued to monitor his activities for the rest of his life.

The controversy over his stand on civil rights ran alongside a related controversy about Armstrong's stage manner. His "jokified" stage persona stemmed from the fact that he came of age, musically and personally, in the era of vaudeville entertainment. Pleasing the audience was paramount.

Most early jazzmen sang, danced, and joked in the spotlight, so it came naturally to him. "You don't pose, never," he once said. "That's the last thing you do, because the minute you pose you're through as a jazzman. Jazz is only what you are."[100]

Armstrong's attempt to please the audience didn't always earn him praise. He was sometimes criticized for his "jokified" stage persona.

Embracing Armstrong Whole

Here, Gary Giddins reflects on the wholeness of Armstrong's art. In his opinion, anyone who disdains his "merely entertaining" qualities will form an inadequate picture.

"A jazz aesthetic incapable of embracing Louis Armstrong whole is unworthy of him, and of the American style of music that he, more than any other individual, engendered. Armstrong was an artist who happened to be an entertainer, an entertainer who happened to be an artist—as much an original in one role as the other.

He revolutionized music, but he also revolutionized expectations about what a performer could be. In the beginning, he was a spur for the ongoing American debate between high art and low. As his genius was accepted in classical circles around the world, a microcosm of the dispute took root in the jazz community, centered on his own behavior. Elitists who admired the musician capable of improvising solos of immortal splendor were embarrassed by the comic stage ham. One reason, surely, is that critics were frustrated (far more than Armstrong ever was) by the fact that a relatively few of his fans knew just how profound his stature was."

Some of Armstrong's performances, such as his appearance as a grass-skirted African chief in an early Betty Boop cartoon that included live action, today seem naive and embarrassing. But by the standards of their time, his performances were not unusual.

In his life and work, Armstrong was never anything but dignified and fair. Besides, he'd been a showman since the days when he sang for pennies in the streets of New Orleans. As Gary Giddins puts it, "He was as much himself rolling his eyes and mugging as he was playing the trumpet."[101]

Armstrong hated the idea that jazz belonged only to black people. As he puts it, "How do we know who copied what?"[102]

He made a point of keeping his band mixed, even when it cost him jobs. He knew that the strength of jazz lay in its universal appeal.

Armstrong's insistence on noninvolvement in politics can be seen as a political statement. Lester Bowie, a distinguished trumpeter and political activist, remarks in a 1986 interview:

The revolutionary that's out waving a gun in the streets is never effective—the police just arrest him. But the police don't never know about the guy that just smiles and drops a little poison in their coffee. In that sense, [Louis] was a true revolutionary.[103]

Chapter

9 Hello, Dolly! and Goodbye, Ambassador Satch, 1960-1971

Armstrong spent the sixties as a goodwill "ambassador of jazz" for America. The furor that surrounded his statements on civil rights passed, and the U.S. State Department sent him on hugely successful tours around the world. During this period, Armstrong also scored the only Number One song of his lifetime: "Hello, Dolly!"

But the sixties were also difficult. Longtime problems with his health became serious. The decade ended with the death of his manager, Joe Glaser, and a long period of hospitalization for Armstrong. Armstrong refused to stop performing, however, and was planning a new tour when he died in 1971.

Overseas

A series of triumphant European tours in 1955-1956 marked a change in Armstrong's popular image. By the early sixties, he was not just the King of Jazz—he was Ambassador Satch, the bringer of American goodwill.

"Ambassador Satch" performs in the Congo as part of his African goodwill tour. In Africa, Armstrong felt that he had found his spiritual, musical, and familial roots.

The highlight of Armstrong's first African goodwill tour was his concert in Accra, where he played to as many as half a million joyous fans.

Audience reaction in Europe was intense. He even inspired German fans who lived in the communist section of Berlin to sneak across the border. As he recalled later:

> We played in West Berlin . . . and people sneaked over from the East Zone to hear us [although] they wouldn't dare do that for food or anything else. . . . Hardly any of them could speak English, but that didn't bother them or us. The music did all the talking for both sides.[104]

Armstrong's power to move people impressed the European press. This, in turn, influenced the U.S. government, which had not yet been promoting foreign travel by its best-known jazz groups.

State Department officials began to reassess their feelings about jazz and to rethink their attitude about its most famous performer. After all, Armstrong, by now, was better known around the world than almost any other American.

In 1956, he made his first trip to Africa. The highlight was a triumphant concert in Accra, then the capital of the Gold Coast and now the capital of Ghana. The local police estimated one hundred thousand people jammed the outdoor stadium there; a *Life* magazine reporter estimated the turnout at close to half a million.

Armstrong loved Africa. He felt he'd found his spiritual, musical, and familial roots there, and told reporters that he'd come home. "After all," he would say, "my ancestors came from here and I still have African blood in me."[105]

In 1960, he returned to Africa, this time under the auspices of the State Department. The forty-five-concert tour witnessed record crowds at airports and densely packed concerts.

"A Sign of Sanity"

The State Department's gamble paid off handsomely in political feeling. When South African authorities banned him because the All-Stars was mixed black and white, it helped focus attention on that country's segregationist laws. In the Congo, then a new republic suffering from massive fighting, one newspaper called him "a sign of sanity."[106] And in volatile places like Kenya, the universal love that Armstrong radiated helped dispel some of the strong anti-American feelings.

Pop Hits

Armstrong's role as media star continued as well. In 1957, an hour-long TV documentary, narrated by the distinguished newsman Edward R. Murrow, was released. A large retrospective of Louis's music was issued. He recorded two excellent albums with another giant, Duke Ellington. And he collaborated with Dave Brubeck on an ambitious musical, "The Real Ambassadors."

He was also steadily recording new material in search of hits. He succeeded with

All Business

Armstrong always prided himself on being professional and businesslike. In their biography of Armstrong, Max Jones and John Chilton write:

"At rehearsals, on stage and in television studios, he did what had to be done in a businesslike manner. He hated rehearsing, in fact, as most full-time jazzmen do. If it could not be avoided, he saw it through with minimum fuss and maximum good humor. It was an impressive sight to see him saving time and trouble. With musicians he knew, 'rehearsals' generally boiled down to a quick talk over keys and the chorus routine. On TV, a little more is required because of the camera and sound men. Here, when Louis emerged to play his part, he often had the studio 'breaking up.' If he was pushed too hard, though, he could produce an unbeatable streak of stubbornness. When he said, 'that's enough,' the producer could forget about just one more for the lighting crew.

This antagonism towards rehearsals didn't stem from laziness, since he was a persistent worker. We believe it was connected with a fear of disrupting the flow of Armstrong magic. 'I don't go through that and never will,' he protested. 'All these cats can blow and we don't need arrangements.' According to him, all that was needed was agreement on choice of tune and key. Then 'I say "follow me" and you got the best arrangement you ever heard.' Louis was determined not to be dragged down by what seemed to him unnecessarily complicated arrangements, musical or social."

such tunes as "Mack the Knife" and "Blueberry Hill." But the magic Number One that all pop musicians aspire to eluded him until 1964.

When David Merrick, a prominent Broadway producer, approached Armstrong about recording the title song for his new musical, the musician was skeptical. He didn't think "Hello, Dolly!" would go anywhere. Joe Glaser persuaded him to record it, however.

Armstrong dutifully recorded the tune and promptly forgot about it. Then he started noticing that, out of the blue, audiences in even the smaller towns he played were beginning to shout requests for "that Dolly thing." He added it to his repertoire—and just in time.

"Hello, Dolly!" took off like a rocket. It was on the *Billboard* charts for twenty-two weeks and hit Number One in May 1964, knocking the Beatles' "Can't Buy Me

Broadway producer David Merrick hired Armstrong to record the title song for a new musical, Hello, Dolly! *The song rocketed to Number One on the* Billboard *charts—the only Number One song of Armstrong's career.*

Love" out of first place. A hastily assembled album went to Number One in June.

Most jazz purists hated the record, but they had resented Armstrong's journeys into pop for years. Some people, however, saw the tune—and its tremendous success—as vindication for Armstrong. Gary Giddins writes:

> "Hello, Dolly!" was a triumph for [Louis], for his generation, for jazz. . . . The Dolly whom Armstrong so enthusiastically welcomed back was . . . none other than himself— back on top where he belonged.[107]

Armstrong loved the singing of Barbra Streisand, the star of the movie version of *Hello, Dolly!* For a *Playboy* magazine poll that year, he nominated her for all three places in the "best female vocalist" category. He said, "She can sing awhile, can't she? . . . Sings her ass off. . . . Say what you like, Daddy, but she's outswinging every ass this year."[108]

Health Problems

By now, Armstrong was at an age—his late sixties—when most people are content to slow down. Armstrong refused, however, and insisted on maintaining his breakneck pace. Often he traveled in a cramped, underheated bus, which he insisted on using instead of limousines or planes.

He was overweight, and would go on crash diets that worked only temporarily. He was mildly diabetic, still suffering from lip problems, and had an ulcer. As James Lincoln Collier puts it:

> He should have retired to ponder his scrapbook, write his memoirs, and

Armstrong was a great admirer of Barbra Streisand, with whom he appeared in the movie version of Hello, Dolly!

make ceremonial appearances on state occasions. But that was not Louis Armstrong.[109]

He did not lead as unhealthy a lifestyle as many of his musician friends, and he was obsessive about the benefits of laxatives and other herbal medications. Still, he didn't change his bad habits. He drank some and smoked heavily most of his life. Worst of all, his diet was rich and heavy. He loved the foods he'd grown up with—rice, beans, fatty meats.

In Italy in 1959, he suffered a mild heart attack. Even then, he insisted on leaving the hospital after only a week. He went to a Roman club to hear Jack Teagarden's band, stayed up all night with his old friend, then flew back to the states.

A short time later, at New York's annual summertime Jazz Jamboree, he appeared onstage as thousands sang him "Happy Birthday." He told them that Bix Beiderbecke, the great cornetist, had tried to get him for the lead chair in Gabriel's heavenly band. "I couldn't make the gig. It hadn't been cleared with Joe Glaser, the union, or the State Department."[110]

More Problems

Armstrong's physician, Dr. Gary Zucker, got him to start watching his diet and work schedule. Still, in the mid-sixties, Louis developed problems with his leg veins as well as shortness of breath. He was hospitalized several times, but refused to retire. Dr. Zucker remarks, "If he couldn't make music then he was through, and life wasn't worth living."[111]

In 1969, a tracheotomy was performed to help his chronic lung problems, despite concern that the surgery would affect his voice. The surgeon who performed this operation, Dr. Moses Nussbaum, said later, "I want to tell you, one of the most frightening days of my life was when I had to put the tracheotomy into Louis Armstrong."[112]

Armstrong poses with Dean Martin on Martin's television show in 1965. Despite worsening health, Armstrong refused to slow down or take a break from his demanding work schedule.

In June 1969, Joe Glaser suffered a stroke and was admitted to the hospital where Armstrong was recuperating from his operation. Glaser never recovered consciousness and died shortly afterwards. Louis had wanted to visit him in his hospital room, but wasn't well enough himself.

For their December 1969 issue the editors of *Esquire* asked several artists who were nearing seventy to offer advice for the next generation. Armstrong replied:

> Most of your great composers—musicians—are elderly people, way up there in age—they will live forever. There's no such thing as on the way out [as] long as you are still doing something interesting and good. You are in business as long as you are breathing.[113]

At the outdoor Newport Jazz Festival in June 1970, Louis appeared at a concert honoring his seventieth birthday. Despite a downpour, thousands of drenched fans greeted him with a standing ovation. At a party in Hollywood, Armstrong was given a rocking chair in honor of one of his most famous tunes, "Rockin' Chair." Armstrong accepted the gift but scolded the star-studded audience: "I'm not in this stage yet."[114]

The Last Gig

Armstrong was in that stage, but he still kept working. In early 1971, he taped a couple of TV shows, made a record of "The Night Before Christmas" (his last recording), and played a few gigs. One writer dubbed him "the cat with nine lives."[115]

His last public performance was an engagement at the Waldorf-Astoria Hotel in March 1971. Louis's doctor agreed to it on the condition that he stay at the hotel, go downstairs only for the performance, and enter the hospital as soon as it was over.

Armstrong spent the next seven weeks at the hospital before going home to recuperate. While there, he wrote an open letter:

> I'd like to thank all of [my fans] from every nook and corner of the world, for their lovely get-well cards and prayers which did wonders for me. I am looking forward to [getting back on the road]. I feel that I owe them, my public and fans, my services again.[116]

On July 5, Armstrong asked his doctor to help him get the All-Stars together. He was ready to rehearse. On the morning of

July 6, Lucille entered his bedroom at 5:30 A.M. Louis had died in his sleep.

The Funeral

Armstrong's body was put on view at a small nursing home in his neighborhood and then moved to the former Armory in Manhattan. Thousands of mourners came in the next few days to pay their respects.

Armstrong had once said, "When I die, it's gonna be the prettiest funeral you've ever seen. I just wish I could watch it."[117] But Lucille wanted the service to be low-key. The speakers on July 9 at the Corona Congregational Church included

Lucille Armstrong pays tribute to her famous husband at the dedication of his gravestone in 1973. A bronze trumpet sits atop the stone, which is inscribed with the musician's most famous nickname, "Satchmo."

Armstrong on stage with Ella Fitzgerald at the Waldorf-Astoria Hotel in 1971. It was the final performance of his long, illustrious career.

Governor Nelson Rockefeller and Mayor John Lindsay. The pallbearers included Bing Crosby, Pearl Bailey, Frank Sinatra, Ella Fitzgerald, Johnny Carson, and Dizzy Gillespie. Peggy Lee sang the Lord's Prayer.

Armstrong was buried in Flushing Cemetery in Queens with dozens of musicians and thousands of fans in attendance. No traditional marching band led the way, although in New Orleans a group of musicians gathered shortly after his death. The parade and memorial service there drew fifteen thousand people.

Stung by Louis Armstrong

Lucille continued to live in the house in Corona. She died in 1983, as she was about to receive a citation from Massachusetts governor Michael Dukakis. Louis's second wife, Lil, with whom he had remained cordial, died in Chicago in 1971—while performing at a memorial service for him. In 1987, the Armstrong house was taken over by Queens College, and plans are being made to turn it into a state landmark.

Armstrong never had children, but his legacy lingers on in the generations of musicians he has inspired. One writer, Leslie Gourse, even titled a book about jazz singers to reflect this: *Louis' Children.*

Most people remember Armstrong as a joyous, clowning entertainer. Not many are aware of the stunning influence he had on music. As his friend, trumpeter Max Kaminsky, once remarked, "I still don't think he's got the appreciation he deserves. Maybe in a hundred or two years from now they'll know how great he really was."[118]

Tony Bennett, one of the greatest interpreters of American popular songs and jazz, sums it up this way:

Every musician I know who's worked in popular music or jazz music has been "stung" by Louis Armstrong. The

With his jovial stage manner and innovative music, Armstrong pleased audiences like no other.

A Japanese sign welcomes Armstrong to an Osaka theater in 1954. Armstrong was a universal entertainer, loved by fans around the world.

bottom line of any country is, what have we contributed to the world? And *we* contributed Louis Armstrong.[119]

Trumpeter Miles Davis, famous for being stingy with his praise, once remarked, "You know, you can't play anything on a horn that Louis hasn't played."[120]

He had an impact far greater than within a single community of performers. As Wynton Marsalis, one of the best contemporary trumpeters, puts it:

> He was a man who was truly universal. He was loved in Africa, he was loved in Europe, he was loved in Japan—everywhere he went, not just because he smiled . . . but because the sound of that horn was a pure, spiritual essence —the sound of America and the freedom that it is supposed to offer.[121]

Armstrong's recordings are still strong sellers, especially since compact-disc technology has revealed new delights in hard-to-hear early recordings. He was even a chart-topper after his death: "What a Won-derful World," from the soundtrack of *Good Morning, Vietnam*, became a hit in 1988.

Looking back, it seems as though Armstrong was ready-made to become an icon for America. He was born, as legend would have it, on the Fourth of July. He raised himself up despite terrible odds. He came of age at a time when the world was looking to America as the source of bold new ideas, and he became a brilliant generator of those ideas.

The fact that he was black, at a time when blacks everywhere were just beginning a long struggle for equality, made him even more notable. He was famous, rich, and influential. But he also suffered, because of his skin color, his attitude, or his occasional outspokenness.

Throughout it all, Armstrong remained remarkably true to himself and to his art. And he somehow stayed humble. As he once put it, "All I want to do is live— good or bad, just live. . . . If I get poor, I'll still be happy. Like I always say, it's better to be 'once was' than 'never was.'"[122]

Notes

Introduction: This Music Called Jazz

1. Quoted in Albert McCarthy, *Louis Armstrong*. New York: A.S. Barnes & Co., 1959.
2. Quoted in McCarthy, *Louis Armstrong*.
3. Gary Giddins, *Satchmo*. New York: Doubleday/Dolphin, 1988.
4. Giddins, *Satchmo*.

Chapter 1: Armstrong's Early Life, 1901-1914

5. Gary Giddins, "Satchmo's Nursery," collected in *Faces in the Crowd*. New York: Oxford University Press, 1992.
6. Quoted in James Lincoln Collier, *Louis Armstrong: An American Genius*. New York: Oxford University Press, 1983.
7. Louis Armstrong, *Satchmo: My Life in New Orleans*. New York: Prentice-Hall, 1954.
8. Armstrong, *Satchmo: My Life in New Orleans*.
9. Quoted in Collier, *Louis Armstrong: An American Genius*.
10. Louis Armstrong, *Louis Armstrong—A Self-Portrait*. New York: The Eakins Press, 1966.
11. Quoted in Max Jones and John Chilton, *The Louis Armstrong Story*. Boston: Little, Brown & Co., 1971.
12. Armstrong, *Louis Armstrong—A Self-Portrait*.
13. Quoted in Giddins, *Satchmo*.
14. Quoted in Giddins, *Satchmo*.
15. Armstrong, *Satchmo: My Life in New Orleans*.

Chapter 2: A Star in New Orleans, 1914-1922

16. Quoted in Collier, *Louis Armstrong: An American Genius*.

17. Quoted in Jones and Chilton, *The Louis Armstrong Story*.
18. Quoted in Jones and Chilton, *The Louis Armstrong Story*.
19. Armstrong, *Satchmo: My Life in New Orleans*.
20. Armstrong, *Satchmo: My Life in New Orleans*.
21. Armstrong, *Satchmo: My Life in New Orleans*.
22. Armstrong, *Satchmo: My Life in New Orleans*.
23. Armstrong, *Satchmo: My Life in New Orleans*.
24. Armstrong, *Satchmo: My Life in New Orleans*.
25. Armstrong, *Satchmo: My Life in New Orleans*.
26. Giddins, *Satchmo*.

Chapter 3: The Beginnings of Fame, 1922-1925

27. Collier, *Louis Armstrong: An American Genius*.
28. Quoted in Jones and Chilton, *The Louis Armstrong Story*.
29. Quoted in Arnold Shaw, *The Jazz Age: Popular Music in the 1920s*. New York: Oxford University Press, 1987.
30. Quoted in Jones and Chilton, *The Louis Armstrong Story*.
31. Jones and Chilton, *The Louis Armstrong Story*.
32. Collier, *Louis Armstrong: An American Genius*.
33. Shaw, *The Jazz Age: Popular Music in the 1920s*.

34. Quoted in Jones and Chilton, *The Louis Armstrong Story.*

35. Quoted in Jones and Chilton, *The Louis Armstrong Story.*

36. Quoted in Giddins, *Satchmo.*

37. Quoted in Jones and Chilton, *The Louis Armstrong Story.*

38. Quoted in Jones and Chilton, *The Louis Armstrong Story.*

39. Quoted in Giddins, *Satchmo.*

40. Quoted in Jones and Chilton, *The Louis Armstrong Story.*

41. Quoted in Jones and Chilton, *The Louis Armstrong Story.*

42. Quoted in Jones and Chilton, *The Louis Armstrong Story.*

43. Quoted in Collier, *Louis Armstrong: An American Genius.*

44. Giddins, *Satchmo.*

45. Quoted in Collier, *Louis Armstrong: An American Genius.*

46. Quoted in McCarthy, *Louis Armstrong.*

47. Jones and Chilton, *The Louis Armstrong Story.*

Chapter 4: Return to Chicago, 1925-1929

48. Quoted in Jones and Chilton, *The Louis Armstrong Story.*

49. Quoted in Giddins, *Satchmo.*

50. Quoted in Giddins, *Satchmo.*

51. Quoted in Collier, *Louis Armstrong: An American Genius.*

52. Giddins, *Satchmo.*

53. Giddins, *Satchmo.*

54. Quoted in Collier, *Louis Armstrong: An American Genius.*

Chapter 5: Broadway and Beyond, 1929-1932

55. Quoted in Giddins, *Satchmo.*

56. Quoted in Jones and Chilton, *The Louis Armstrong Story.*

57. Quoted in Jones and Chilton, *The Louis Armstrong Story.*

58. Quoted in Jones and Chilton, *The Louis Armstrong Story.*

59. Quoted in Giddins, *Satchmo.*

60. Quoted in Jones and Chilton, *The Louis Armstrong Story.*

61. Collier, *Louis Armstrong: An American Genius.*

62. Collier, *Louis Armstrong: An American Genius.*

Chapter 6: Consolidating a Career, 1932-1943

63. Quoted in Jones and Chilton, *The Louis Armstrong Story.*

64. Collier, *Louis Armstrong: An American Genius.*

65. Armstrong, *Louis Armstrong—A Self-Portrait.*

66. Quoted in Jones and Chilton, *The Louis Armstrong Story.*

67. Quoted in Collier, *Louis Armstrong: An American Genius.*

68. Quoted in Jones and Chilton, *The Louis Armstrong Story.*

69. Jones and Chilton, *The Louis Armstrong Story.*

70. Giddins, *Satchmo.*

71. Quoted in Giddins, *Satchmo.*

72. Quoted in Jones and Chilton, *The Louis Armstrong Story.*

73. Quoted in Jones and Chilton, *The Louis Armstrong Story.*

74. Quoted in Giddins, *Satchmo.*

75. Quoted in Giddins, *Satchmo.*

Chapter 7: The All-Star Years, 1943-1957

76. Giddins, *Satchmo.*

77. Barney Bigard, *With Louis and the Duke.* New York: Oxford University Press, 1986.

78. Quoted in Jones and Chilton, *The Louis Armstrong Story.*

79. Giddins, *Satchmo.*

80. Quoted in Giddins, *Satchmo.*

81. Bigard, *With Louis and the Duke.*

82. Bigard, *With Louis and the Duke.*

83. Bigard, *With Louis and the Duke.*

84. Armstrong, *Louis Armstrong—A Self-Portrait.*

85. Bigard, *With Louis and the Duke.*

86. Bigard, *With Louis and the Duke.*

87. Quoted in Giddins, *Satchmo.*

88. Quoted in Giddins, *Satchmo.*

Chapter 8: Icon and Effigy in Music and Politics, 1957-1960

89. Quoted in Jones and Chilton, *The Louis Armstrong Story.*

90. Armstrong, *Satchmo: My Life in New Orleans.*

91. Quoted in Jones and Chilton, *The Louis Armstrong Story.*

92. Quoted in Jones and Chilton, *The Louis Armstrong Story.*

93. Quoted in Giddins, *Satchmo.*

94. Quoted in Giddins, *Satchmo.*

95. Quoted in Giddins, *Satchmo.*

96. Quoted in Jones and Chilton, *The Louis Armstrong Story.*

97. Quoted in Jones and Chilton, *The Louis Armstrong Story.*

98. Quoted in Giddins, *Satchmo.*

99. Quoted in Giddins, *Satchmo.*

100. Quoted in Jones and Chilton, *The Louis Armstrong Story.*

101. Giddins, *Satchmo.*

102. Quoted in Giddins, *Satchmo.*

103. Gary Giddins, *Satchmo: Louis Armstrong* (video documentary). New York: CBS Music Video Enterprises, 1986.

Chapter 9: Hello, Dolly! and Goodbye, Ambassador Satch, 1960-1971

104. Quoted in Jones and Chilton, *The Louis Armstrong Story.*

105. Quoted in Giddins, *Satchmo.*

106. Quoted in Jones and Chilton, *The Louis Armstrong Story.*

107. Giddins, *Satchmo.*

108. Quoted in Jones and Chilton, *The Louis Armstrong Story.*

109. Collier, *Louis Armstrong: An American Genius.*

110. Quoted in Jones and Chilton, *The Louis Armstrong Story.*

111. Quoted in Collier, *Louis Armstrong: An American Genius.*

112. Quoted in Collier, *Louis Armstrong: An American Genius.*

113. Quoted in Giddins, *Satchmo.*

114. Quoted in Collier, *Louis Armstrong: An American Genius.*

115. Quoted in Jones and Chilton, *The Louis Armstrong Story.*

116. Quoted in Giddins, *Satchmo.*

117. Quoted in Jones and Chilton, *The Louis Armstrong Story.*

Epilogue: Stung by Louis Armstrong

118. Quoted in Jones and Chilton, *The Louis Armstrong Story.*

119. Giddins, *Satchmo: Louis Armstrong.*

120. Quoted in Albert McCarthy, *Louis Armstrong.*

121. Quoted in Giddins, *Satchmo: Louis Armstrong.*

122. Armstrong, *Louis Armstrong—A Self-Portrait.*

For Further Reading

Louis Armstrong, *Satchmo: My Life in New Orleans*. New York: Prentice-Hall, 1954. A little disingenuous, as many autobiographies are, but simply written and entertaining. Takes Armstrong through his childhood and early playing experiences until the time he leaves for Chicago to join King Oliver's band. Armstrong was working on another volume of memoirs when he died. There is some evidence that Joe Glaser and others (maybe Lucille) had a hand in sanitizing this book—Armstrong made many references in interviews to wanting to someday get his story down right, the way he really wanted it told.

James Lincoln Collier, *Louis Armstrong: An American Genius*. New York: Oxford University Press, 1983. The most exhaustively researched and detailed biography, but a little inaccessible for the general reader by the overflow of information (especially technical information on musicianship). Highly opinionated, but detailed and generally astute chapters on Armstrong's huge volume of recordings. Contains some inaccuracies (especially about Armstrong's early years) later corrected by Giddins. Paints a less kind picture of Armstrong than other biographies, indicating he was more insecure, jealous, and paranoid than others would have us believe.

Gary Giddins, *Satchmo*. New York: Doubleday/Dolphin, 1988. Easily the best introduction to further reading about Armstrong. The most accessible and skillfully written of all the biographies (by the jazz critic for the *Village Voice*). Also the most generous-spirited about Armstrong's dual identity as artist and entertainer. Extremely well illustrated with vintage photos and other material. A companion piece to Giddins's documentary film of the same name, available on video (see below). Contains definitive proof about Armstrong's true birth date, not available beforehand.

——— *Satchmo: Louis Armstrong* (video documentary). New York: CBS Music Video Enterprises, 1986. A full-length documentary, including vintage footage and interviews with ex-Armstrong musicians as well as admirers like Wynton Marsalis and Tony Bennett.

Additional Works Consulted

Louis Armstrong: *Louis Armstrong—A Self-Portrait*, originally published as an interview with Richard Meryman that appeared in *Life* magazine, April 15, 1966, reprinted New York: The Eakins Press, 1971. Fascinating—a "monologue" by Satchmo taken from a lengthy interview. Questions have been edited out.

Barney Bigard, *With Louis and the Duke*. New York: Oxford University Press, 1986. An anecdotal memoir by the famous clarinetist, who spent many years with Ellington before joining Armstrong's All-Stars. Opinionated, but with good stories.

Jack V. Buerkle and Danny Barker, *Bourbon Street Black: The New Orleans Black Jazzman*. New York: Oxford University Press, 1973. A fascinating look at the world of New Orleans jazz using extensive oral history and anecdotes from over fifty musicians, some famous and some not. Buerkle is a sociologist, Barker a lifelong resident of New Orleans and musician. Dryly written, but the oral histories are vivid.

Gary Giddins, "Satchmo's Nursery," collected in *Faces in the Crowd*. New York: Oxford University Press, 1992. An essay-length version of Giddins's book-length biography, collected in a book of essays about a variety of musicians, actors, and writers.

Robert Goffin, *Horn of Plenty: The Story of Louis Armstrong*. New York: Da Capo, 1977. (Reprint of 1947 edition published by Allen, Towne & Heath, New York). A very early and often inaccurate biography by a Belgian jazz writer. Full of hilarious and completely invented dialogue, mostly embarrassing dialect: "'Willy,' said Mary suddenly, "taint no two ways 'bout it—we's gwine leave this heah mizzable dump!'" According to Giddins, Armstrong made extensive notes for Goffin as he was preparing this book, but Goffin made little use of them. Giddins also thinks Goffin was badly served by his translator. Important only as a socio-historical phenomenon.

Max Jones and John Chilton, *The Louis Armstrong Story*. Boston: Little, Brown & Co., 1971. Written by two British early-jazz fanatics soon after Armstrong's death. A little too personal to be trustworthy, and poorly organized, but with some good anecdotes, especially of Armstrong's early European tours.

Albert McCarthy, *Louis Armstrong*. New York: A.S. Barnes & Co., 1961. For the hard-core musicologist; primarily a detailed analysis of Armstrong's music, especially the recorded work. But also a short biography with a few good details not found in the primary works. Suffers from having been written by an overly polite Britisher.

Nat Shapiro and Nat Hentoff, *Hear Me Talkin' to Ya: The Story of Jazz by the Men Who Made It*. New York: Rinehart, 1955. Transcribed interviews and anecdotal oral histories.

Arnold Shaw, *The Jazz Age: Popular Music in the 1920s*. New York: Oxford University Press, 1987. Has a chapter on King Oliver and Armstrong. Written by a music professor.

Index

Credits

About the Author

Adam Woog is a freelance writer and the former jazz critic for the *Seattle Times*. He is distantly related to the Karmofsky family, who gave Louis Armstrong his first job. Woog writes often about his native Pacific Northwest, including the books *Sexless Oysters and Self-Tipping Hats: 100 Years of Invention in the Pacific Northwest* and *Atomic Marbles and Branding Irons: Museums, Collections, and Roadside Curiosities of Washington and Oregon*. He has written several books for Lucent Books including *The United Nations* and *The Importance of Harry Houdini*. Woog lives in Seattle, Washington, with his wife and daughter.